1001
unbelievable
FACTS

1001 unbelievable FACTS

Mind-boggling, impossible, weird...

Helen Otway

ARCTURUS

ARCTURUS

This edition published in 2008 by Arcturus Publishing Limited
26/27 Bickels Yard, 151–153 Bermondsey Street,
London SE1 3HA

ISBN: 978-1-84837-132-3

Design & Illustration by quadrum■

Printed in Singapore

CONTENTS

1001
Unbelievable
Facts

Have you ever stopped to think about all the unbelievable things
that are going on in the world? In the time it's taken you to read
that sentence, hundreds of unimaginable things have just
happened…and that's hard to believe too!

Even before there were people on the planet to decide whether
something was unbelievable or not, a whole range of unimaginable
stuff was going on. *Tyrannosaurus rex*, for example, had incredible
jaws full of foot-long teeth that were strong enough to crush a car!
Then there was the gigantic *Brachiosaurus* – it was the length of two
buses and weighed at least 35 tonnes (77,161 pounds)!

As soon as people came along, they would often spend their days
looking for crazy things to do, ranging from making fire with a
couple of sticks to building huge structures without any machinery
whatsoever. Over time, scientists came out as the champions of
inconceivable truths and often made unbelievable discoveries
without even meaning to!

Rubber duck facts:

(Free extras, not part of your 1001 facts!)

You don't have to be a scientist to do something unbelievable, of course. Doing something simple like collecting rubber ducks is incredible too…if you have more than 2,580, like world record holder Charlotte Lee. Here are some other things you probably don't know about rubber ducks:

Queen Elizabeth II has a rubber duck that wears a crown! After this flabbergasting fact was revealed in the media in 2001, UK rubber duck sales increased by 80 per cent.

150,000 rubber ducks took part in the largest ever rubber duck race in Dublin in 2006.

Thousands of rubber ducks were lost from a tanker during a Pacific storm in 1992 and were washing up all over the world for more than a decade afterwards. Their movements have provided valuable information about ocean currents.

Over to you

However dumbfounded you are by the time you reach the end of this book, reward yourself by writing down your own incredible fact to reach the 1001 target. It could be something that happened to you, like forgetting your own birthday, or something that you saw on the news, like the plans for a new type of paper to be made from panda poo!
Get ready to believe one thousand unbelievable facts…because they're all true!

Don't go there!

Run the 100 metres as many times as you like and see how your time compares to the world record. Study the nearest newborn baby and check if he or she really does blink only once or twice a minute (clapping your hands to make them blink doesn't count). But please, please, please don't try any of the dangerous stuff mentioned in this book. Whenever you ride your bike, for example, keep your hands on the handlebar at all times and don't try and take it through any tunnels of fire, okay? Be sensible and you'll live to see another unbelievable day!

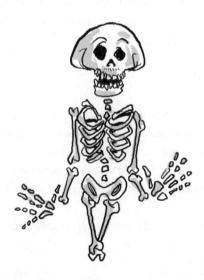

Unbelievable
Body Facts

Whether your hair is curly or straight depends on the shape of your hair follicles: curly hair grows from oval follicles, straight hair grows from round follicles.

The average human body is made up of more than 50 trillion cells.

A Michigan couple opened a parcel delivered to their home and were shocked to find a liver and an ear inside! The parts should have been delivered to a nearby research laboratory.

Retrieving a memory takes 0.0004 seconds.

You have no control over some of your muscles! These are known as *involuntary muscles* that the body uses for functions like breathing and digesting food.

If you're right-handed, you tend to chew food on the right side of your mouth; if you're left-handed, you tend to chew on the left.

Tooth enamel is the hardest substance in your body.

An operation on a patient in a Belgrade hospital was disrupted when two surgeons started a fight! They took their punch-up outside and the assistant surgeon completed the procedure.

There are hundreds of viruses that can give you a cold. That's why there is no cure!

Haemochromatosis is a hereditary iron overload disorder – iron accumulates in the body, damaging the organs and darkening the skin.

Your brain is your hungriest organ!
20 per cent of what you eat feeds it.

The painkilling drug aspirin comes from willow bark and was first described by Hippocrates in the 5th century BC.

A British pensioner who lost her false teeth discovered that her dog had eaten them! The dog had a 3-hour operation to have them removed.

Red blood cells are made inside your bones. Each cell travels around the body about 250,000 times before it returns to the bone marrow to die.

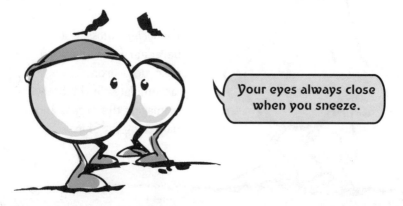

Your eyes always close
when you sneeze.

Sometimes a muscle fully contracts by itself when you're not expecting it and is very painful – that's cramp!

Your digestive system will process around 50 tonnes (110, 231 pounds) of food in your lifetime.

Wreaths, pictures, jewellery and postcards that are made of or contain human hair are on display in Leila's Hair Museum, Missouri. These keepsakes were commonly made in Victorian times.

Florida girl Jennifer Mee hiccupped continuously for five weeks! The hiccups stopped as suddenly as they had started.

One person in 20 has an extra pair of ribs.

In an emergency, your body will produce a hormone called *adrenaline* that gives you superhuman strength!

Pain signals reach the brain more slowly than touch signals. That's why rubbing things better really works!

There are more than 700 kinds of bacteria lurking in your large intestine.

Astronauts have to wear a *maximum absorption garment* when they go on spacewalks. That's right, just like a baby!

You have more than 230 joints in your body.

An eyebrow hair lasts for only 10 weeks, whereas a hair can stay on your head for five years.

Some infections lead to *strawberry tongue*, in which the bumps on the tongue swell up, making it look like a strawberry.

On average, right-handed people live nine years longer than left-handed people!

Some of your muscles can contract and relax again in a fraction of a second, such as those in your eyes.

You use 72 muscles when you talk. That's quite a workout!

The growing obesity problem has led to one British council installing bigger furnaces in its crematoriums that can hold 1-metre (3 feet) wide coffins.

Long, thin cell structures in your fingernails make them rip across, not downwards.

Abnormal skin cells can be frozen away. Liquid nitrogen causes instant frostbite on healthy skin, but is often used to get rid of warts and moles.

Men are more likely to be colourblind than women.

You are hairy all over! Only your lips, palms and soles of your feet have no hair on them – the rest of your body is covered in around five million hairs.

Your heart beats more than 30 million times each year!

An Indian man sold one of his kidneys…to raise money for a trip to the 2007 World Cup Cricket match in the West Indies.

You have a stirrup, an anvil and a hammer in each ear! They are tiny bones that were named in a time when there were more blacksmiths around than there are today.

Any part of your body can be removed and replaced with a machine, except your brain.

The lining of your stomach completely replaces itself every three days.

You lose 47 per cent of your body's heat from your head. That's why you should wear a hat if it's chilly.

The only animal that can get a sunburn, apart from a human, is a pig.

You could live for a month without food, but only a week without water.

In ancient Greece, a prisoner called Histiaeus sent his son-in-law a secret message to start a rebellion...by tattooing it onto his slave's head!

Your thighbone or *femur* is the longest bone in your body.

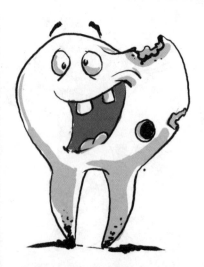

Early American toothpaste boxes from 1968 were black and featured an x-ray picture of a decayed tooth. Marketing has improved a little since then!

You have six million *cones* in each eye! They are the cells that make you see colours.

Long distance swimmers eat while they're in the water to keep up their energy levels.

The hormone that makes you grow is produced only when you sleep, so if you want to be taller you should go to bed when you're told!

Women blink almost twice as much as men.

The ancient Greeks believed that a sneeze was a good sign from the gods. In parts of India, it is believed to be a sign of good health!

Fingernails grow four times more quickly than toenails.

African-American singer Screamin' Jay Hawkins was famous for a song called 'Constipation Blues'.

Each nerve cell in your brain can receive over 100,000 messages a second!

A Yemeni man was found to have four kidneys instead of two. Although he was offered money for his spare ones, he decided that they were a gift from Allah and kept all four.

A red blood cell takes less than a minute to go round your whole body!

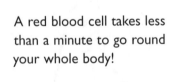

Your hair grows more quickly in warm weather than in cold weather.

A New Zealand tree surgeon broke his leg near the top of a 40-metre (130 feet) high tree... and was then injured further when the rescue helicopter swung him into another tree!

Your body is made up of 66 per cent water.

There are 100,000 hairs on the average human head.

Babies and children blink less often than adults. Newborn babies blink only once or twice a minute!

Your lungs are different sizes! The left one is smaller to make room for your heart.

Your skull is made up of 22 bones.

A Chinese man has grown the nails on his left hand for 15 years, so that their total length is more than 1 metre (3 feet). He avoids crowded places in case one of them gets broken!

Japanese women have the highest average life span and can expect to live beyond the age of 80.

Your thyroid gland is butterfly-shaped. It's in your neck and makes important substances that make you grow and develop properly.

Children and young adults need twice as much oxygen as people over 80 years of age.

Someone who forgets a word or name during conversation is suffering from *lethologica*.

Your gallbladder is dark green!

Ever wondered what that little pink lump in the corner of your eye is? Our ancestors had an extra eyelid that would close horizontally to protect the eye. We haven't needed it for thousands of years, so it has disappeared through evolution.

More than half of your bones are in your hands and feet.

Brain cells are the only cells in the body that do not regenerate. When they're gone, they're gone!

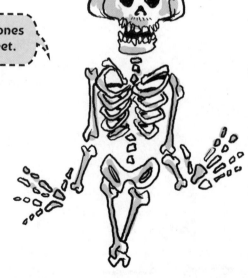

A 1956 Olympic water polo match between Hungary and the USSR was abandoned after it degenerated into an underwater brawl.

The skin is thickest on the soles of your feet and gets thicker if you walk around barefoot a lot. The skin is thinnest on your eyelids.

Every tiny move you make uses muscles – you have more than 630 altogether!

A hair follicle on your head will rest for up to 6 months after a hair falls out before a new hair sprouts out of it!

Ancient philosophers believed that mental activity took place in the heart.

Your brain was as big as an adult's when you were just 6 years old!

It is possible to live without your large intestine.

Your nose helps you to taste things! That's why it's difficult to taste your food if you have a cold and can't smell anything.

A Brazilian woman who had suffered from stomach pain for years was finally given an X-ray...that revealed a scalpel inside her body! The surgical tool had been left there 23 years earlier when she had given birth by caesarean section.

Dead bodies are stored in a morgue at a temperature of 2-4 degrees Celsius (35-39 degrees Fahrenheit).

Forensic scientists can identify a person's age, gender, race and state of health from a single hair.

Gold can reduce swelling and is given to arthritis sufferers by injection.

As you're reading this, 4 per cent of your blood is in your heart. The rest is whizzing around your body!

Salivating before throwing up is the body's way of protecting your teeth from the high acid levels in vomit.

A Dutch gym runs naked workout sessions. Ewww!

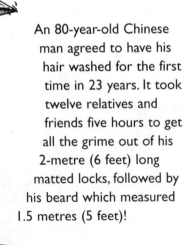

An 80-year-old Chinese man agreed to have his hair washed for the first time in 23 years. It took twelve relatives and friends five hours to get all the grime out of his 2-metre (6 feet) long matted locks, followed by his beard which measured 1.5 metres (5 feet)!

The liver is your largest internal organ – it has more than 500 functions and has two blood supplies.

The fingerprints of koala bears and humans are so similar that they could be confused at a crime scene.

There are seven types of stool listed on the Bristol Stool Chart medical aid, ranging from 'separate hard lumps, like nuts' (Type 1) to 'entirely liquid' (Type 7).

You have an amazing nose! It's so sensitive that it can tell the difference between 10,000 smells.

You will walk the equivalent of five times round the world during your lifetime!

Nerve signals are super fast! It takes less than one hundredth of a second for a nerve signal from your toe to reach your brain.

Women and children breathe more quickly than men.

A Polish car thief was tracked down after he left his false teeth at the crime scene! Police used dental records to catch the culprit.

The human body is at its lowest ebb between 3am and 4am – the most likely time for someone to die in their sleep.

The older you are, the more quickly your nails will grow.

Even though your gastric juices are acidic enough to dissolve metal, you cannot digest tomato seeds – they pass straight through your intestines.

Although they weigh a lot less, your bones are as strong as steel.

Your largest muscles are the ones you sit on! You have a *gluteus maximus* in each buttock.

Humans babies are born without kneecaps.

99 per cent of the body's calcium is in your bones and teeth.

Laughing and coughing put more pressure on your spine than standing or walking do. Some people have even developed back injuries from coughing.

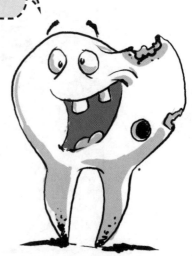

Touching the soft palate at the back of your mouth triggers a gag reflex, but this can be controlled with practice – sword-swallowers train themselves to resist it.

Your kidneys take just four minutes to clean all the blood in your body.

Your small intestine is covered with tiny finger-like projections called *villi*. They increase the surface area of your intestine to absorb the maximum amount of nutrition from food.

Some of your muscles stretch to twice their resting length when you exercise!

When you cough, the air rushes through your windpipe faster than the speed of sound.

One in 600 people are born with *Horseshoe kidney*, where the two kidneys have joined together to make a horseshoe shape.

By the time you feel thirsty, your body is already dehydrated.

Humans have a tailbone! Its proper name is the *coccyx*, which means cuckoo – it got its name because it looks like a cuckoo's beak.

Your nails are naturally thick or thin – nothing can make them thicker, whatever the claims on nail cosmetics may say!

We are the only animals that cry tears when we are upset.

85 per cent of people can curl their tongue into a tube. The other 15 per cent get annoyed that they can't.

Poisons in the body can be stored in the hair shaft for years, even after death.

Your ears and nose carry on growing throughout your whole life.

You have the same number of bones in your neck as a giraffe has. The difference is obvious…giraffe bones are a lot longer!

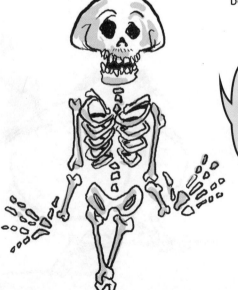

Your bones are alive! If they weren't full of living cells, they wouldn't be able to mend themselves when they get broken.

You lose your sense of smell as you get older, so children can smell far more than their parents or grandparents.

The nail on your middle finger grows more quickly than the others.

Surgeons trying to correct the limp of a 5-year-old boy in China lengthened the wrong leg! The confusion arose when the boy was anaesthetised whilst lying on his back and operated on whilst lying on his stomach. Always best to check!

The deadly anthrax virus can live for years at room temperature. Luckily, it's not very common.

You spent the first half hour of your life as a single cell.

Your body is producing *cerebrospinal fluid* all the time! The fluid acts as a cushion to protect your brain and constantly needs replacing.

Babies under one month old do not cry tears.

A person with a cold sprays up to **40,000** infectious droplets into the air when they sneeze!

Synaesthesia is a condition where two senses overlap. Russian artist Wassily Kandinsky, for example, perceived musical notes as colours.

Hair and fingernails are made from the same substance, called *keratin*.

You are slightly taller in the morning than you are when you go to bed.

Identical twins have the same DNA but different fingerprints.

One type of E coli causes food poisoning, but there are hundreds of strains of the bacteria – you have some in your intestine!

Professional athletes have a very slow resting heart rate.

Fatal insomnia is a rare inherited illness where sufferers get so little sleep that they eventually waste away and die.

The skull is much softer at birth to allow the brain to grow – newborn babies often have misshapen heads!

A lack of the mineral *iodine* in the diet causes a big lump in the neck when the thyroid gland swells up.

Your heart first started beating three weeks after you were conceived.

You dream for around two hours a night.

The US has the highest rates of obesity in the developed world – two thirds of its adults are classed as overweight or obese.

Lung Pinprick Condition is a rare condition in which microscopic holes appear in the lungs.

The 8th March is World Kidney Day…how will you celebrate?

Your muscles are made up of bundles of muscle fibres – each one is as thin as a hair.

10 per cent of people have a protruding belly button, or an *outie*. Whether you have an *innie* or an *outie* depends on the shape and size of your umbilical cord when you were born!

Foetuses sometimes have hiccups and also suck their thumbs…but probably not at the same time.

Your voice is unique! No two people have exactly the same larynx, nose and mouth shape, so your voiceprint is all yours.

Some people are born without an appendix. That saves them the trouble of having it out later...

Your eye muscles work really hard – they make around 100,000 movements in a day.

Men have larger brains than women – but women have more brain cells!

The brain cannot sense touch or pain, so brain surgery can be done while the patient is still awake! If a tumour is being removed, a surgeon may talk to the patient to check for alertness and that the operation is not damaging healthy parts of the brain.

You have water in your bones! Twenty per cent of your skeleton is made up of water.

Unbelievable Food Facts

Early bubble gum was pink because it was the only food colouring available at the time.

Doughnuts originally had a nut in the centre.

An Italian woman was cleaning the soil from potatoes for dinner when one turned out to be a hand grenade! Neighbours called the police and the weapon was safely detonated.

Mice are a delicacy in Zambia and Malawi.

A New York restaurant offers the ultimate luxury pizza, topped with lobster and six kinds of caviar. It's a bargain at $1,000 (£600)!

Canadian sculptor Cosimo Cavallaro sprayed a whole house with... cheese! He used 4,500 kilograms (9,920 pounds) of cheddar to cover the house inside and out.

Boiling a lobster alive is a crime punishable by a fine in northern Italy.

African-American scientist George W. Carver invented over 100 products made from peanuts, including cloth dyes and wood stains.

Sausages were invented thousands of years ago as a way of preserving and eating all the nasty-looking leftovers from slicing up an animal into cuts of meat.

Mexicans love chocolate sauce...on turkey!

Fifteenth-century candy canes were not cane-shaped, but straight. Their curved shape came from a 17th-century priest who reshaped the candy so that it resembled shepherds' staffs.

The United States is the world's largest producer of cheese.

Vinegar eels are tiny worms that can be found in vinegar. Don't worry – bottled vinegar is pasteurised and filtered, so you won't find any wriggling around on your chips!

During the 19th century, lard (pig fat) was used as a spread, like butter.

If glacé cherries did not have red colouring added, they would be beige.

The glue on Israeli postage stamps is certified kosher.

Japanese artist Tatsumi Orimoto goes around the world's cities and shakes hands with people... with baguettes strapped to his head, covering his face! He calls his performances *Bread Man*.

The mango comes from the same family as poison ivy – its skin can irritate the mouth if eaten.

Tea was originally a medicine in ancient China.

Witches' broom fungus and *frosty pod rot* are fungi that affect cacao plants, the plants used to make chocolate.

Welshman Captain Beany worships baked beans! He dresses in baked bean orange, bathes in beans and formed the New Millennium Bean Party.

You cannot use fresh pineapple in a jelly – it contains an enzyme that stops it setting.

Tomatoes are berries.

A Mumbai businessman caused outrage when he opened the Hitler's Cross restaurant, where diners were greeted by a huge picture of the Nazi leader.

Black salt is actually pinkish grey!

Garlic has long been used for its medicinal properties and was an ancient Egyptian cure for worms and tumours.

Watermelons grow wild in the Kalahari Desert.

More people are allergic to cows' milk than any other food.

Marshmallow got its name from the plant of the same name. The first marshmallows contained the plant extract as its gelling agent, but modern forms use gelatine. This makes them unsuitable for vegetarians, as gelatine is made from boiled up animal parts!

Poppy seeds contain the painkilling drug morphine and are banned in Singapore for this reason.

Carrot jam is a delicacy in Portugal.

Grapefruits got their name from the way they grow in clusters, looking like bunches of huge grapes!

Dried peas have been found in Egyptian tombs.

Dozens of people from northern India became fatally ill in 1998 after using what they thought was mustard oil in their cooking. It was discovered that the oil had been made from poisonous prickly poppy seeds, which look and taste like mustard seeds.

Black Magic and *Black Beauty* are types of aubergine.

A British girl put two shop-bought organic eggs in an incubator to see if they would hatch. A few weeks later, two fluffy chicks popped out!

Turkeys originally came from Mexico. Their English name comes from the fact that they were first brought to England from Turkey.

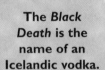

The *Black Death* is the name of an Icelandic vodka.

Popcorn was discovered thousands of years ago by Native Americans, who enjoyed popcorn soup and popcorn beer.

Until the 18th century, English people believed tomatoes were poisonous.

Basil seed drink with honey is a thick, seed-filled Asian drink. Drinking it is said to be like drinking frogspawn!

Forbidden rice is a black rice grain that becomes dark purple when cooked and turns the water it is cooked in bright purple.

Salad Blue and *Blue Congo* are types of potato. Anyone for blue fries?

Drinking grapefruit juice can be dangerous when taking medication, as it allows chemicals to build up in the body.

Slices of bacon were known in the sixteenth century as *collops*. Christians would eat meat before Lent on Collop Monday.

The lovely smell of lemons can help you concentrate! A study using the citrus aroma in cars showed that both male and female drivers performed much better than they did without it.

Coca-Cola was originally green.

There are more than 350 different types of pasta.

Honey is antibacterial and never goes off.

The British are big tea fans – the average Brit drinks 23 times more tea than the average Italian!

It takes more calories to digest a piece of celery than there are in the celery itself. No point in eating that then!

26 million eggs are eaten in the UK every day. That's an eggstraordinary amount!

Lens is Latin for lentil – the lenses in your eyes are lentil-shaped!

A Chinese car dealer covered a Volkswagen Beetle in 200 kilograms (440 pounds) of chocolate for his Valentine's Day display!

Hedgehogs were eaten in medieval times and are still a source of food in some countries. One way to cook it is in clay – when the baked clay is broken off, the hedgehog spines come with it.

Popular Korean snack *beondegi* are silkworm pupae that have been steamed or boiled and then seasoned. They sound delicious!

The cucumber originally came from India.

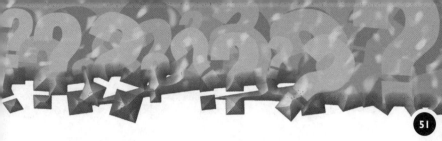

A meal survey showed that the average Briton eats spaghetti bolognese 3,000 times in their lifetime.

Cashew nuts come from cashew apples!

Throwing celery on to the pitch is a tradition for fans of the English football team Chelsea. Even so, it has recently become a criminal offence and one arrested fan vowed never to eat celery again!

The remains of 4,000-year-old noodles were found at a site in China in 2005, settling the argument of where they were invented!

There are more chickens in the world than any other bird.

Salt was highly prized by the Romans – soldiers were sometimes paid in salt, which is how the word 'salary' originated.

The first ketchup was made with pickled fish in East Asia.

For one of his exhibitions, designer Jean-Paul Gaultier had dresses, shoes and hats specially made...by bakers! His show was called *Pain Couture* and the exhibits were made from bread and pastry.

During the Middle Ages, children were given beer for breakfast!

The average British household throws away almost a third of the food it buys.

A Welshman celebrated the opening of his new pizza takeaway shop by having a slice of ham and pineapple pizza tattooed on the back of his head! His tattoo took three hours and the event raised money for charity.

Fruits with *choke* in their name are sour and difficult to swallow, such as the choke pear and chokecherry.

Watermelon rinds are edible and are used as a vegetable in Asian stir-fries and stews.

Brazil nuts only grow in rainforests.

An English fisherman saved an edible crab…because it had three claws! Instead of ending up as lunch, Claudette the mutant crustacean went on show at the local aquarium.

The Mount Horeb Museum in Wisconsin has a collection of over 4,000 different types of mustard.

The first coffee was sold in chemists' shops and was known as *Arabian wine*.

A Chinese man fed instant noodles to his dogs too often – they became addicted and refused to eat anything else!

The largest chicken egg recorded had five yolks in it!

The tea in tea bags is the waste product left over from the sorting of higher quality loose-leaf tea – it's known as *dust*.

There are no turkeys eaten in Turkey.

Japanese chocolate comes in fiery-hot *wasabi* flavour!

Until the 17th century, all carrots were purple. Now you can choose to eat orange, red, yellow or white ones too!

Roman Emperor Nero liked his iced desserts!
He would send slaves to the mountains to fetch snow,
which would then be mixed with fruit, nuts and honey.

Chickpeas were used as a coffee substitute during the First World War.

A British man with a food phobia has lived mainly on cheese for 20 years. The only other things he can bear to eat are crisps!

Banana plants have been used to make cloth for hundreds of years in Japan.

Eggshells contain calcium and are sometimes used as a food additive.

Puffed rice is made from grains of rice that have been heated until they bubble up to produce thin outer walls. The noise you hear when you pour milk onto your cereal is those walls collapsing from the moisture!

Medieval wafers were made with coats-of-arms imprinted on them.

Vietnamese snake wine is a large bottle of rice wine...with a cobra coiled up inside it! It is sold for its medicinal properties.

Aubergine is also known as *eggplant* because some types are not purple but white, and as the fruits are growing, they look like eggs!

In Poland and Germany, the last Thursday before Lent is known as *Fat Thursday*, when people stuff themselves with cakes!

Until 2004, chewing gum was banned in Singapore.

A can of cola contains the equivalent of seven teaspoons of sugar.

Former North Vietnamese President Ho Chi Minh once worked as a pastry assistant in the kitchens of London's Carlton Hotel.

Despite being a cancer-causing substance, talcum powder is still used in some countries to coat rice to improve its appearance. Talc-coated rice is banned in the USA.

Peanut oil can be used to make paint, varnish, polish, insecticides, soap and explosives.

People train *pig-tailed macaque monkeys* to collect coconuts in parts of Asia.

Milk for US President William Taft and his family was provided by a cow that grazed freely on the White House lawn!

It takes 40 minutes to hard-boil an ostrich egg!

Until the 20th century, lobster was seen as a food for the poor and was even used as fertilizer!

The poisonous plant *hemlock* has a large white root and can be mistaken for wild parsnip…with disastrous results!

A medieval Christmas dinner would consist of swan or peacock.

The Australian *finger lime* has the widest colour variation of any citrus fruit — it can be green, red, orange, yellow, purple, black or brown!

Garlic that has been stored in oil for too long can produce the highly toxic poison *botulism*.

Dogs have been eaten in China for thousands of years.

Trenchers were medieval plates made from stale bread. When the meal was finished, the trenchers would be given to the poor to eat. How generous!

Frost is necessary in the growing of parsnips. It helps to develop the flavour.

Bubble tea or *pearl tea* is an Asian tea drink that comes in different flavours. What makes it unusual is that it has big, black, chewy *tapioca* balls swimming around in it that lurk at the bottom of the cup!

The strawberry is the only fruit that has its seeds on its outer skin.

The Romans used to eat lettuce as a dessert.

The *horned melon*, also known as the *African horned cucumber*, has a jelly-like flesh that tastes like a cross between a cucumber and a kiwi fruit.

Italian *cibreo* is a sauce made from cockscombs and chicken livers.

French soups sold in the street were called *restaurers* for their restorative properties. The first restaurant opened in Paris in 1765, selling the soups and providing tables to eat them at.

A rotten egg has a green yolk.

The amount of rice that rice *blast fungus* destroys each year could feed 60 million people.

Strawberries and red peppers both contain more vitamin C than oranges, weight for weight.

China is the world's leading producer of apples.

Snail-spitting champion Alan Jourden can spit a snail 9.4 metres (31 feet). Competitors have a run up before they spit out their mollusc as far as they can.

Peanuts are widely eaten in China and India, but peanut allergy is rare there.

Eggs 'n' brains is a southern USA dish made with scrambled eggs and pig's brain. Yummy!

Before industrialized food production, one big noodle would be cooked for a meal in Chinese households – it was considered bad luck to cut it before it was served.

A *craisin* is a dried cranberry.

People in central Europe used to rub garlic on their chimneys and keyholes to keep away vampires and werewolves.

Cheese was invented in around 8000 BC.

Ancient Romans used to breed dormice for food. One dormouse made a tasty starter.

There are more Maltese people in Melbourne, Australia, than there are in Malta.

Guanciale is Italian cured pig's cheek.

Some Indonesian men drink cobra blood to make them more manly. King cobra blood is the most expensive!

Coffee was originally banned in some countries because it was considered addictive.

White hens lay white eggs.

The first cheesecakes were served at the ancient Greek Olympic games more than 2,000 years ago.

The *turpentine mango* smells of…turpentine! It is safe to eat, but the experience is said to be like eating a regular mango in a freshly painted room.

90 per cent of Cambodia's agricultural land is used to grow rice.

Nineteenth-century English geologist William Buckland claimed to have eaten his way through the animal kingdom, including panther and crocodile. He said the worst things he had tasted were mole and Bluebottle jellyfish.

No species other than humans drink milk from the mothers of other species.

Eating large amounts of carrots will turn your skin orange.

It takes 40 litres (88 pints) of sap from a maple tree to make 1 litre (2.2 pints) of maple syrup.

Chicken neck skin is sometimes used as a casing for kosher sausages.

Artist Gayle Chong Kwan has made sculptured landscapes from food. Her works have included puffed rice walls, mashed potato mountains, cheese buildings and a ham tower.

Abbeville, Louisiana, has a Giant Omelette Celebration in which a 5,000-egg omelette is made in a giant pan.

Sliced bread was invented in 1928 in Missouri, USA.

Candy canes first became peppermint flavoured with red and white stripes in Sweden in the 19th century.

A *fuzzy melon* is an Asian vegetable similar to squash.

Kangaroo meat is very low in fat – kangaroo sausages, known as *kanga bangas*, and kangaroo steaks are available in Australia.

Japanese scientists believe chewing gum is good for your brain. Chewing stimulates the learning centre of the brain and can actually improve your memory!

A chicken can lay more than 200 eggs a year.

The early Catholic church banned sausages as they were traditionally eaten during pagan festivals.

Fried cod tongues are a popular Norwegian dish.

Fortune cookies were invented in California.

Ankimo is a Japanese delicacy of steamed monkfish liver with the veins removed.

There is no ham in a hamburger. The name comes from the fact that the first meat patties served in a bread bun were made in Hamburg, Germany.

Unbelievable Animal Facts

A woodpecker's tongue can be as long as its body! It has a barb on the end of it for skewering grubs. Yummy!

Large rodents called Agoutis are the only animals that can open brazil nuts with their teeth.

Insects first appeared 300 million years ago, even further back in time than dinosaurs.

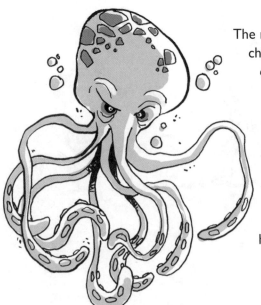

The mimic octopus can change its shape and colour to look like other sea creatures. It can even make itself long and thin to do an impression of a sea snake!

Locusts can fly for 20 hours without stopping.

Osedax mucofloris is a slimy sea worm that feeds on whale remains and looks like a flower growing from the bone it's eating. Its name means 'bone-eating mucus flower'!

The eyes of a hamster blink independently of one another.

A flamingo always feeds with its head upside down.

Austrians were puzzled when they found a dead shark on a freshwater riverbank. A chef eventually confessed – he had put it there as a joke when it began to smell as he defrosted it for a buffet!

Meerkats are immune to many deadly venoms and will eat scorpions...stinger and all!

New Zealand fisherman caught a colossal squid that was 10 metres (30 feet) long. Its body was so enormous that *calamari rings* (squid rings) made from it would be as big as tractor tyres!

It can take a month for the contents of a sloth's stomach to digest completely.

The United States and Russian armies have trained dolphins to rescue lost divers and seek out underwater mines.

A giant anteater gobbles up around 3,000 ants and termites in one day, using its sticky tongue that can be as long as 60 centimetres (2 feet)!

Beavers have a set of transparent eyelids to protect their eyes as they swim underwater.

Some fish can walk! Mudskippers can survive on land and have strong fins that they use as legs to get around.

The strongest leather comes from ostrich skin.

Workers at a Kenyan animal sanctuary were surprised when an orphaned baby hippo chose Mzee the 130-year-old giant tortoise as its new parent! Since Owen the hippo was rescued from the sea after the 2004 tsunami, the pair have lived, slept and played together.

Chemicals taken from *Kamchatka* crabs have been used to treat burns.

In the same way that people are right or left-handed, elephants are right- or left-tusked!

Staff at a British zoo had to hand-feed milk to a baby *colobus monkey* after it was rejected by its mother…for having hiccups!

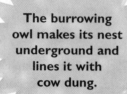

The burrowing owl makes its nest underground and lines it with cow dung.

Polar bears have transparent (not white!) hair and their skin is black to absorb maximum heat from the sun.

Hippos, whales and dolphins are the only mammals that give birth under water.

Bees have five eyes!

Birds can eat berries that are highly poisonous to humans.

Fuji the dolphin put on weight after having her diseased tail amputated because she couldn't swim properly. Handlers at the Japanese aquarium came up with a speedy solution – a new tail was made from the material used for Formula One racing car tyres!

The total combined weight of the world's ant population is heavier than the weight of the human population.

The greater bulldog bat likes to go fishing! Its super sonar detects the slightest of ripples…then it swoops down to catch the fish in its sharp wing claws!

More than 40 per cent of all mammal species are rodents.

Both male and female octopuses die shortly after mating.

Mexican police discovered 132 wild animals in the boot of a coach, after investigating strange noises. Some toucans, iguanas, parrots, snakes and turtles were confiscated but none of the passengers would admit to owning them. So no arrests were made!

Snakes have no taste buds.

The only fruit eaten by aardvarks is known as the *aardvark cucumber*. African Bushmen call it *aardvark dung*!

Dalmatians are genetically disposed towards deafness. Until this was discovered, they were thought to be plain stupid!

Frogs do not drink water; they absorb it through their skin.

An elephant's tummy makes lots of noise when it's digesting food, so elephants can stop their digestion at will if there's any danger of a predator hearing it!

A stag's antlers are made of bone.

Dachshund means 'badger dog': the dogs were originally bred for killing badgers, rabbits and foxes. Not so cute, then!

Chalkbrood is a fungal disease that destroys honeybee larvae and gives them a chalky white appearance.

Owls are far-sighted, so they cannot see things close up very clearly.

Austrian mechanics soon discovered the cause of a squeak in a tourist's car: a kitten trapped above one of the wheels! The kitten was shaken but had survived the car's 1,500-kilometre (900-mile) journey.

Squirrels can climb trees faster than they can run on the ground!

Adult swordfish have no teeth.

An armadillo can stay underwater for up to 6 minutes! First it fills its stomach with air; otherwise it would sink under the weight of its heavy body-armour.

Bat bugs look like bed bugs and suck the blood of bats.

A pair of storks made a nest in the middle of a German golf course and filled it with golf balls. They're probably still waiting for them to hatch!

A male *kodiak* bear on its hind legs is gigantic: over 3 metres (10 feet) tall.

Newborn rattlesnakes have no rattle! The bead needed to make the rattle noise in their tail does not form until they have shed their first skin.

Some starfish are circular. They must feel a bit out of place…

Crabeater seals don't eat crabs! They eat *krill*, tiny shrimp-like creatures.

Until 1997, the punishment for killing a panda in China was death.

A giant catfish frightened divers in a Dutch holiday park. The monster fish was found to be 2.3 metres (7 feet 6 inches) long and ate three ducks a day, but staff promised that it wouldn't eat people!

Bedbugs and fleas can live for a whole year without eating.

A spider monkey's tail is so strong that it can pick fruit with it!

The African pygmy mouse gets water by stacking pebbles in front of its burrow and drinking the dew from them in the morning.

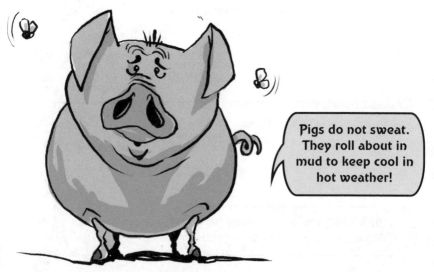

Pigs do not sweat. They roll about in mud to keep cool in hot weather!

The African pancake tortoise has a flat, soft shell…just like a pancake! The shell is no use against predators, but it does help the tortoise to avoid them by enabling it to hide in narrow crevices.

Both the coat and the skin of a tiger are stripy.

Birds' eyes are fixed in their sockets, so they have to move their whole head to look at something – try it yourself, keeping your eyes still!

The colour of a flamingo comes from all the shrimp it eats. A pale flamingo is not getting enough food!

The male four-horned antelope is the only mammal with four horns.

When unravelled, the thread of a
single silkworm's cocoon can
be a kilometre (over half a
mile) long.

A queen
termite can live
for 15 years.

Two smelly musk hogs were
married in a lavish ceremony
in Taiwan to celebrate the
Year of the Pig. The pigs were
dressed up for the occasion and
even got to scoff some wedding cake!

The roadrunner is a type of cuckoo. Some Native American
tribes believed that it protected against evil spirits.

Lions are colour blind –
that's why a zebra's
camouflage is so
effective!

A German farmer found a novel way of protecting his sheep from hoof infection: he kitted out his flock in special little Wellington boots!

Male lions spend most of their time resting and are inactive for around 20 hours a day.

A seal was found over 6 kilometres (4 miles) from the sea, struggling down a country lane in Lancashire, England. How it got there is still a mystery!

Elephants have only four teeth that can be replaced up to six times in their lifetime.

The colourful St Andrew's Cross spider is so called because it rests in its web with its legs outstretched in an x formation.

Sharks are covered in sharp, tooth-like scales called *denticles*.

The tapir has a long snout that is *prehensile* – that means it can move in all directions and grasp things!

The Harpy eagle is so large and powerful that it can easily carry away a monkey in its talons.

Phonetics experts have discovered that birds chirp with regional accents!

The call of a blue whale is louder than a jumbo jet and can be heard 800 kilometres (500 miles) away.

A cat's nose has a unique print, just as your fingerprints do!

If a shark is turned upside down it will go into a state of paralysis, known as *tonic immobility*, for up to 15 minutes.

A group of owls is known as a *parliament*.

Tarantulas cannot spin webs.

An elderly Swedish woman took animal rescue a little too far: police found that she had been sheltering 11 swans in her tiny Stockholm apartment for more than five years!

Snakes are an example of *obligate carnivores*: all they eat is meat, meat and more meat!

There are 18 different kinds of piranha fish, but only four of them are dangerous.

Unlike other big cats, cheetahs cannot roar. They can purr, though!

A rat can go without water for longer than a camel.

If you find a *mermaid's purse* washed up on the beach, it is the empty egg case of a dogfish, skate or maybe even a shark!

A tiny tree frog wandered into the freezer of a café in Darwin, Australia, and was found frozen solid. Once thawed out, though, it was fine. (Maybe it had only gone in for a croaka cola…)

Amphibian skin absorbs chemicals as well as water, so a frog sitting in an anaesthetic solution will quickly go to sleep.

West African woolly bats are so tiny that they live in spiders' webs.

A German cat was sent through the post after sneaking into a parcel while its owner looked for more tape.

Brazilian police went to investigate an abandoned truck and discovered five lions inside it! Each of the lions had to be fed 10 kilograms (22 pounds) of meat a day until their owner could be found.

Snails can sleep for three years.

The postman caterpillar eats poisonous leaves. It feeds on cyanide-filled passionflower leaves and stores the poison in its spikes to put off predators.

Sea urchins have been on the planet for around 450 million years.

Big, fat atlas beetle larvae can bite when touched.

A new bakery that opened near Frankfurt, Germany, offered treats such as tuna cakes and garlic cookies...just for dogs!

200 cats brought to a Chinese village to get rid of the rat problem were rewarded for their hard work with an enormous fish banquet!

No two zebras have the same stripy pattern.

A cow who lost part of her leg when she broke it in a fall was saved from slaughter when her owner had a false one made. Now she can move fine!

A parrotfish's teeth continue to grow throughout its life.

The platypus and the echidna are the only two mammals that lay eggs and give their young milk.

One pat of elephant dung can contain up to 7,000 dung beetles!

Cats hate the smell of oranges and lemons.

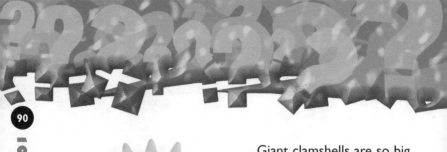

Giant clamshells are so big that in the past they have been used as children's baths and church fonts.

A North American *caribou* deer will travel up to 5,000 kilometres (3,000 miles) in a year.

Sea pigs are a type of sea cucumber: they live in really deep oceans, rolling around in the mud on the seabed and eating it!

Pandas cannot digest bamboo very well, but they still spend all day eating it – 98 per cent of what they eat is bamboo!

A male African elephant weighs as much as 170 men.

An Australian crocodile was so annoyed by the sound of a chainsaw nearby that it ran at the man using it and grabbed it from him!

An oyster can be male one year and female the next!

A rhinoceros's horn is not a true horn – it's made of matted hair.

Whales have been found with circular scars on their skin – marks from the suckers of giant squid.

The coconut crab, or robber crab, lives on land and will drown in water.

Giraffes, camels and cats are the only animals that walk by moving both their left feet together, then both their right feet together.

Some shrews have red teeth! The strange colour comes from iron deposits.

Swordfish have special organs in their heads that heat up their eyes and brain.

A cow caused an accident by wandering into a road in Columbia and was punished by being put into prison.

Owls cannot turn their heads right round. They can turn them further than you can, though – to an angle of 135 degrees in each direction.

A horse in Coventry, England, was found to have hay fever! Teddy, the horse's owner had to give him shredded newspaper to sleep on instead.

Pandas have unusual paws that look like hands with a thumb and five fingers on each.

The *tarantula hawk* is actually a wasp! The female attacks and paralyses a tarantula so that she can lay her egg on its body. The hatched larva then eats the tarantula alive.

The powerful jaws and sharp teeth of a snapping turtle can rip off a person's finger.

King snakes, such as the king cobra, eat other snakes.

A cat's heart beats twice as fast as a human's!

There is a rare armadillo in Argentina that is small and pink – its name is the *pink fairy armadillo*!

Rodents are immune to the rabies virus.

If it has no food, a ribbon worm can eat up to 95 per cent of its own body to survive.

An adult mayfly lives for only one day. It doesn't even get chance to eat anything, as it spends all its time mating and laying eggs.

Siberian Huskies can live and work in temperatures as low as minus 60 degrees Celsius (minus 75 degrees Fahrenheit).

Parrotfish can make themselves a kind of mucus sleeping bag! It masks their smell from predators and keeps parasites away.

Not all penguins live in cold climates – the Galápagos penguin lives near the equator.

Pit vipers are so called because of the holes between their nostrils and eyes that contain heat sensors. They track down prey in the dark by detecting the difference in temperature between an animal and its background. The sensitive heat detectors can pick up a difference in temperature of less than 1 degree Celsius (33.8 degrees Fahrenheit)!

Pea crabs are tiny crabs – the size of peas, in fact!

Black bears have been known to take the lids off jars and undo door latches.

Giant sea stars are starfish that can have an arm span of more than 60 centimetres (24 inches)! They can be brown, green, red or orange.

> Odd-eyed cats have one eye that is blue and one eye that is green, orange or yellow.

Sloths eat, sleep and give birth upside down. They are held in place by their sharp claws and will even stay hanging from a branch after they have died!

Penguins have a filter above their eyes that converts saltwater to freshwater. The excess brine drips out of their bills and sometimes they sneeze it out!

> A starving mouse will eat its own tail.

The honey possum is a tiny Australian marsupial that is half the size of a mouse and feeds entirely on pollen and nectar.

Dolphins have no sense of smell. They can see and hear very well, though.

Basenji dogs have unusually shaped larynxes and do not bark – they make a yodelling sound!

A shark's liver makes up around a quarter of its body mass. It's so huge because it provides the buoyancy that other fish get from gas-filled swim bladders.

Anteaters are the only mammals that have no teeth.

A four-legged duckling was born on a duck farm in Hampshire, England. The farm owner named him Stumpy.

If you gently scratch a koala's fur, your fingers will smell of eucalyptus – their favourite food!

When it attacks prey, the great white shark rolls its eyes backwards to protect them.

The fierce grasshopper mouse will defend its territory by howling like a little wolf!

Bats always turn left when they fly out of a cave.

Unbelievable History Facts

Nineteenth-century British Prime Minister William Gladstone was once injured in an attack by a cow during a country walk.

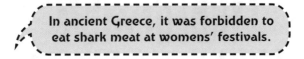

In ancient Greece, it was forbidden to eat shark meat at womens' festivals.

The remains of Louis IX of France are in more than one place: some of his entrails were buried where he died in Tunis, others are in Palermo and one of his fingers is in Paris. The rest of his body went missing in the 16th century.

Richard I of England (also known as Richard the Lionheart) died from an arrow wound that became gangrenous.

Before coins were invented, shells were used in many countries as money.

The murder rate in the Middle Ages was around ten times higher than it is today.

The *Slinky* toy was invented in the early 1940s after US engineer Richard James dropped a torsion spring and thought its movements were fun!

One of the first glues was made by the ancient Egyptians...from boiled up animal skins!

The first factory-produced toilet paper became available in 1857 in the USA. People used all sorts of things before that – anything from leaves and fruit skins for the poor to lace or wool for the rich!

The first five Tarzan films were silent. No Tarzan calls in those, then...

Nelson Mandela's first name was Rolihlahla, but his teacher could not pronounce it and chose Nelson for him instead, after Horatio Nelson.

Arctic explorer John Hornby died of starvation after trying to spend a year without supplies by the Thelon River.

The ancient Egyptians were the first to establish a 365-day year.

The 3 mile (5 kilometre) long tomb of Chinese emperor Qin Shi Huangdi contains more than 8,000 life-size clay soldiers, created 2,300 years ago to protect him in the afterlife.

Gustave Eiffel originally intended to build his famous tower in Barcelona for the 1888 Universal Exposition, but his idea was rejected.

The tug-of-war was an Olympic Games event between 1900 and 1920.

Fourteenth-century traveller John Mandeville wrote that the cotton plant 'was a wonderful tree which bore tiny lambs on the ends of its branches'!

Ancient Egyptians shaved their heads to keep cool in the heat and to prevent getting lice.

Many 19th-century artists and writers living in Paris were fond of a green alcoholic drink called *absinthe*, also known as 'the green fairy'. It was believed to be dangerously addictive and cause madness, so was banned in most countries by 1915.

The *Titanic* sank in 1912, but its wreck was not discovered until 1985.

Charlie Chaplin anonymously entered a 'Charlie Chaplin look-alike' competition and didn't win any prizes at all!

The careers of many stars of silent movies collapsed with the arrival of the 'talkies' – movies with sound.

Leo II became the Byzantine Emperor in 474 when he was just seven years old!

Furnaces beneath the floors of buildings provided central heating systems in ancient times.

Jimmy Carter was the first US President to be born in a hospital.

During the Ming Dynasty, important officials wore belt buckles carved from the beaks of hornbill birds.

The first man on the moon, Neil Armstrong, was travelsick as a child.

New Zealand mountaineer Sir Edmund Hillary spent his early adulthood being a beekeeper.

A popular form of art in medieval Russia was the carving of walrus tusks.

Christopher Columbus was not the first European explorer to reach the Americas. He had to abandon his 1492 voyage when his ship ran aground, and didn't get there until 1498 – by which time others had beaten him to it!

Mozart wrote his first piece of music when he was just five years old.

Clipperton Island is a ring-shaped island with a lagoon in the middle that was named after an 18th-century pirate.

A *lyre* was an ancient Greek musical instrument made from a tortoise shell and some antelope horns.

Vikings used to drink from the skulls of their defeated enemies.

Neither of Joseph Haydn's parents could read music. That didn't stop him becoming one of the world's most famous composers though!

In 1863, a naughty boy called Santiago Ramóny Cajal was locked up for destroying his town's main gate with his homemade cannon. He went on to become a top scientist!

The Chinese invented fireworks more than 2,000 years ago. The sound was created to scare off evil spirits.

Deer antlers were used in the Stone Age to make harpoons, axes, combs and needles.

Popes normally wear a tiara made from gold or silver for their coronation, but in 1800 Pope Pius VII had to wear one made from papier maché! The French Republicans had just stolen all the good ones.

The mummy of Siptah showed that the young Egyptian ruler had a severely deformed foot.

Ernest Hemingway had a cat with six toes.

Before high-speed drills were invented, dentists used slow hand drills on their patient's teeth. Ouch!

Native American tepees were originally made from animal skins.

The bullet that killed Admiral Horatio Nelson is on display in Windsor Castle, England.

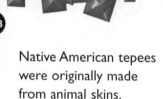

The hair from a young Roman's first shave would be offered to the gods. Emperor Nero put his in a lovely gold box with some pearls!

French artist Henri de Toulouse-Lautrec broke both his legs in his early teens and they stopped growing. As an adult, he had a fully-grown torso and child's legs.

Surveyor JG Tierney drowned whilst looking for a suitable site for the Hoover Dam on the Nevada/Arizona border. Exactly 13 years later, his son died in a fall at the construction site of the dam.

Construction of Barcelona's unique *Sagrada Familia* cathedral began in 1883 and it still isn't finished! Work is due to be completed in 2026.

During the Second World War no Olympic Games were held.

Ancient Chinese coins were rectangular with a hole in the middle. The hole was for stringing them together.

The first helicopter flight lasted 20 seconds, with the rotary wing aircraft managing to get 30 centimetres (1 foot) off the ground!

India has not invaded another country in the last 10,000 years of history.

12 million African slaves were taken to the Americas before the trade was banned in 1808.

Within the space of 77 years, the Russian city of St Petersburg had its name changed to Petrograd, then Leningrad, then back to St Petersburg again.

The owl was a symbol of death for the Aztecs, Mayans and ancient Romans.

Dr Mary Edwards Walker became the first female US Army surgeon in 1863. She went on to fight for women's dress reform and was arrested several times for wearing men's clothing.

Early concrete was made with volcanic ash.

Some ancient tribes used animal dung to stiffen their hair. And you thought gel was stinky!

Legendary American Olympic gold-medallist Jesse Owens died of lung cancer after smoking for 35 years.

All of Queen Anne of Great Britain's 18 children died before the age of 12.

Sunglasses were worn in China as long ago as the 12th century, using pieces of smoky quartz as dark lenses. They were worn more to conceal facial expressions during interrogation rather than for protection against the sun!

Alexander the Great ordered his soldiers to shave off their beards in case the enemy used them as a handle to grab hold of!

Marilyn Monroe worked in an aeroplane parts factory before she became famous.

US President Woodrow Wilson's wife Edith was a descendent of Native American Pocahontas.

The FA Cup is the oldest football competition. The first final was in 1872 between teams called the Wanderers and the Royal Engineers. The Wanderers won 1-0!

Nineteenth-century French writer Guy de Maupassant disliked the Eiffel Tower so much that he would often have lunch in its restaurant…so he wouldn't have to look at it!

The Volskwagen *Beetle* car was designed for Adolf Hitler by Ferdinand Porsche.

The sister ship of RMS *Titanic* was to be called *Gigantic*, but its name was changed to *Britannic* after the disaster involving the first ship. *Britannic* sunk too after hitting a mine in 1916.

King Henry VIII's first wife was chosen for him when he was 11 years old, following his brother's death. He was to marry his brother's widow when he was old enough.

In ancient times, children were considered to be grown-ups around the age of 12. They were expected to give up any toys to the Gods.

French aviator Henri Fabre made the first seaplane in 1910. The strange invention flew tail-first and was called *Le Canard* – The Duck!

US President William Howard Taft was a big man. So big, in fact, that he kept getting stuck in the White House bath and a larger one had to be installed.

Until the 18th century, it was considered unmanly to eat with a fork.

Winston Churchill was born in a ladies' room in Blenheim Palace when his mother went into labour during a dance.

Argentina was named in the 16th century. The country is rich in silver, so the name came from the Latin for silver, *argentum*.

Hollywood icon James Dean starred in only three films. Tragically, he died in a car crash aged 24.

Beer is one of the oldest drinks and was even enjoyed by the ancient Egyptians!

Ancient anatomists believed that the arteries transported air through the body. Blood pools in the veins after death, so the arteries of a corpse seem empty.

Alan Shepard was the first astronaut to play golf on the moon.

Champagne was invented in England, not France.

The shape of a pyramid represents the rays of the sun falling to Earth. The step formation was designed so that the dead Pharaoh inside could walk up to heaven on the sunrays!

Murderous dictator Idi Amin gave himself the snappy title 'His Excellency President for Life, Field Marshal Al Hadji, Dr Idi Amin, VC, DSO, MC, Lord of All the Beasts of the Earth and Fishes of the Sea, and Conqueror of the British Empire in Africa in General and Uganda in Particular.'

The first elevator shaft was invented four years before the elevator!

African-American Rosa Parks started a mass civil rights movement in 1955 when she was arrested for refusing to give up her bus seat for a white man.

Greek fire was a weapon used by the Byzantine Greeks in naval battles. A stream of burning fluid that couldn't be put out with water was fired at enemy ships.

In 1893, New Zealand became the first country to allow all its women to vote.

> Only 48 hat tricks have been scored throughout the FIFA World Cup's history. There were none scored during the 2006 tournament, but eight were scored in 1954!

The lead in pencils has never contained lead! Pencils were developed from graphite sticks, which were used in the 16th century to mark sheep, and the first ones had casings made from string or sheepskin.

The Romans built 85,000 kilometres (53,000 miles) of roads across their empire. That's a lot of digging!

The first hardhat was known as a 'hard-boiled hat' and was made from canvas hardened with glue and black paint.

Early false teeth were made from hippopotamus bone and dead people's teeth!

The 1938 radio broadcast of H.G. Wells' *The War Of The Worlds* caused panic amongst many listeners who believed that aliens really had landed!

John F. Kennedy could read so quickly that he often got through two or three books a day. He could speak quickly too and held the record for fastest public speaker.

Soviet cosmonaut Valentina Tereshkova was the first woman in space in 1963, but it was another 19 years before the Russians allowed another woman to fly up there!

The first affordable car, the Ford Model T, had a top speed of 45 miles(72 kilometres) per hour and worked with a single pedal.

Viking celebratory feasts could last for ten days!

Nineteenth-century Scottish explorer James Augustus Grant suffered severe swelling to his leg whilst in Africa and was given a hot poultice made from cow dung, salt and mud from the lake. It would have taken his mind off the pain, if nothing else!

Wealthy ancient Egyptians were embalmed in honey when they died.

The fire that started after the 1906 San Francisco earthquake caused more damage than the earthquake itself did.

The Boab Prison Tree is a huge, hollow tree that was used to lock up prisoners on their way to Derby, Australia, during the 19th century.

Seventy nations were involved in the Second World War.

When the nudes in Michelangelo's Sistine Chapel paintings were considered too shocking, another artist was asked to paint clothes over the offending parts!

St Paul's Cathedral in London has been built and rebuilt at least five times.

Sixteenth-century aristocrat Lucrezia Borgia had a hollow ring that stored poison for use in her enemies' drinks.

Ancient Greek engineer Archimedes invented the first luxury ship in the 3rd century BC. Large enough to carry 600 people, it had a garden, a temple and even a gym!

J.R.R. Tolkien's *The Lord Of The Rings* trilogy took 12 years to write. Tolkien's day job was as an Oxford University professor.

Lightning struck the Eiffel Tower in 1902, damaging the monument's top 100 metres (328 feet).

Frederick the Great preferred the company of his greyhounds to people and wanted to be buried next to them when he died. His successor Frederick William II was having none of it and had him buried next to his father!

Victorian postmen in England wore red tunics and were known as robins.

The best-known Tarzan actor, Johnny Weissmuller, was an Olympic gold medal-winning swimmer and set 67 world records in swimming during the 1920s.

The remains of Christopher Columbus started off in Valladolid and were moved several times to Seville, Santo Domingo, Havana and back to Seville again!

The Chauvet Cave in southern France contains cave paintings that are more than 30,000 years old.

British Prime Minister Lord Palmerston was often late for appointments – even dinner with Queen Victoria!

Ancient Greek perfume containers were such shapes as helmets and sandalled feet. Today's perfume bottles are a little more romantic!

Seventeenth-century aristocrat Prince Rupert of The Rhine took his large poodle dog into battle with him on several occasions.

People only began to celebrate Christmas more than 400 years after Jesus Christ died. Later, under Oliver Cromwell, it was made illegal for more than a decade.

The Tower of Pisa took 174 years to build, and it was never even straight to begin with!

Seventeenth-century bottles of champagne exploded so frequently that cellar workers had to wear iron masks for protection.

Nineteenth-century American poet Emily Dickinson wrote more than 1,700 poems but less than a dozen were published in her lifetime.

The waxy-looking embalmed body of Soviet leader Vladimir Lenin has been on show in Red Square since he died in 1924.

Heavy snow slowed down the normally accurate Big Ben clock in London on New Year's Eve 1962, making it announce the New Year ten minutes late.

The first living beings to go up in a hot air balloon were a sheep, a duck and a rooster in 1783.

Henry VIII decided that because she couldn't give him a son, his second wife Anne Boleyn must have been a witch!

Polish-American pianist Józef Hofmann had such small hands that he had to use a specially made piano with narrow keys.

Until 1984, there were no television programmes broadcast during the month of July in Iceland. What on earth did they do instead?

French novelist Victor Hugo also produced more than 4,000 drawings in his lifetime, sometimes using coffee or soot.

The first ever newspaper was printed in 1605 and looked like a book.

Gerald Ford was the longest-living president, living to the age of 93 years and 165 days.

Can openers were invented 50 years after tin cans.

The Nobel Peace Prize is named after Swedish chemist Alfred Nobel – the man who invented dynamite.

Early pens were made from animal bone.

A steeplejack did a parachute jump from the top of New York's Statue of Liberty in 1912.

American inventor Thomas Edison proposed to his wife in Morse code!

Levi Strauss invented jeans in the 1850s when he saw a need for hardwearing trousers amongst miners. His first versions were made with sailcloth, then he imported a French material called *serge de Nimes*… which became shortened to denim.

The first Mercedes car was named after a company executive's daughter.

Even ancient Greek babies had rattles – hollow clay shapes had bits of clay inside to make the rattle sound.

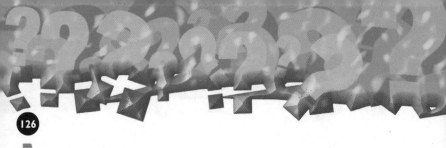

Louis XIV became King of France at the age of 4 and went on to reign for 72 years.

Mystery surrounds the death of American writer Edgar Allan Poe – he was found wandering the streets in a delirious state, wearing someone elses clothes, and died shortly afterwards.

The first job of British naturalist and explorer Alfred Wallace was as a builder.

The name Wendy was not used before the publication of J.M. Barrie's *Peter Pan*.

Italian composer Antonio Vivaldi started off as a violin teacher and was once sacked from his job!

Alfred Nobel's studies on explosives tragically caused the death of his brother Emil in an explosion.

American astronaut Buzz Aldrin's mother's maiden name was Moon.

Yellow tennis balls were not used at Wimbledon until 1986. Before that they were white.

Sugar Ray Robinson was one of the greatest boxers of all time, winning his first 40 fights as a professional.

Danish physicist Niels Bohr made his escape from the Nazis in 1943 in a fishing boat.

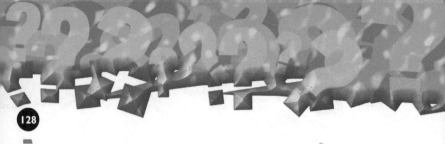

The first lighthouse was built in 285 BC near Alexandria, Egypt. The light was created by a fire that had to be kept burning all night!

Five workers died during the construction of the Empire State Building in New York.

Nelson Mandela was the oldest elected President of South Africa, taking office at the age of 75.

Viking coins were valued for their weight. If a Viking had to pay less for something, he would clip a bit off his coin!

Christmas 2004 was the first white Christmas in New Orleans for 50 years.

Unbelievable
Science Facts

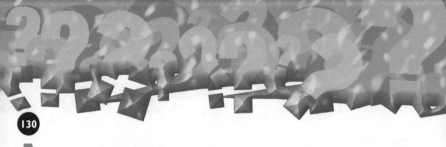

A bolt of lightning is so hot that if it hits sand, it can turn it into glass!

Brazil nut trees can live for more than 500 years.

A trillion tonnes of the world's water evaporates each day in the sun. Luckily, it all comes down again when it rains!

Scientists have created rice that contains human genes! Genetically modified rice was developed with a human liver gene and, more recently, saliva and breast milk proteins.

Dust from Africa and China can end up in North America, getting carried across the sea by trade winds.

Italian astronomer Galileo Galilei was arrested for claiming that the sun was the centre of the universe. His books were also banned by the Catholic Church.

Only one in 1,000 oysters contains a pearl.

The jumping spider does not use big muscles to jump! The energy needed is instead created by a kind of hydraulic system that changes the pressure of its blood and quickly stiffens the legs.

Water is the only substance that occurs naturally in liquid, solid and gas forms (water, ice and steam).

The supersonic airliner Concorde could fly around the world in 31 hours 27 minutes.

The Earth is not completely spherical! It bulges in the middle – if you take a ball and squash it slightly from top to bottom, that is the shape of our planet.

The coldest temperature ever measured on earth was minus 89 Celsius (minus 129 Fahrenheit) at Vostok, Antarctica, on July 21, 1983.

Liquid oxygen is sky blue.

Silver has antimicrobial properties and was used in many treatments before the invention of antibiotics. People would often put a silver coin in their milk to stop it from going sour!

A freak summer hailstorm left Australian capital Canberra under a blanket of ice. In some parts of the city, the ice was up to 1 metre (3 feet) deep!

The gravity on Mars is less than 40 per cent of that on Earth. That means that if you could stand on Mars, you would weigh much less than you do now – instant weight loss!

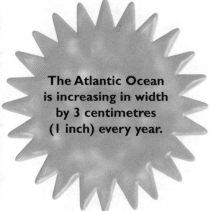

The Atlantic Ocean is increasing in width by 3 centimetres (1 inch) every year.

Scottish biologist Alexander Fleming used multi-coloured bacteria to create germ paintings! The bacteria were invisible as he painted, but became colourful as they grew.

The sun is 4.5 billion years old.

Rainforests cover only 2 per cent of the world's surface, but more than 50 per cent of all our plants and animals are found there.

The largest part of an iceberg is hidden beneath the sea's surface.

Research has shown that deadly pufferfish poison contains cancer-fighting properties and may be used in future treatments.

A hurricane the size of Earth has been raging on Jupiter for the past 300 years!

There is no such thing as moonlight! The light you see is the reflection of sunlight off the moon's surface.

Before the birth of the word 'scientist' in 1833, scientists were known as *natural philosophers* or *men of science*. (Women didn't get much of a look-in back then!)

Mussels, as well as oysters, produce pearls.

There have been no cases of the deadly smallpox virus since 1978, but cultures of the virus are held at the Centers for Disease Control and Prevention in the United States and at the Institute of Virus Preparations in Siberia.

The paper for US dollar bills is made from cotton.

Looking directly at the sun can cause permanent damage to the eye's retina.

Volcanoes produce a kind of natural glass called *obsidian*. It can be formed into a fine cutting edge that is sharper than a steel scalpel blade and is used in cardiac surgery.

The drug used to treat sleeping sickness contains arsenic and kills 10 per cent of patients who receive it.

An exploding star is known as a *supernova* and produces as much energy in a few months as the sun would over billions of years.

There are 500,000 detectable earthquakes around the world each year.

Incandescent light bulbs are extremely inefficient – 95 per cent of the power they use creates heat, so only 5 per cent is used for the light itself.

First-century engineer Hero of Alexandria invented the first vending machine. It dispensed holy water!

British scientist Philip D'Arcy Hart lived until the age of 106 and was still doing research at the age of 100!

The *elasmosaurus* was a prehistoric marine reptile that weighed several tonnes. Its neck was so long that it made up over half its total length of 14 metres (46 feet).

If an ostrich really did bury its head in the sand it would suffocate.

The three main types of meteorite are made of stone, iron or a mixture of the two.

It may look fragile but spider silk is very strong – tougher than steel wire of the same thickness!

Oil is made from the remains of plants and animals that lived millions of years ago. That's why it could eventually run out.

Peat moss can hold up to 20 times its dry weight in water, a bit like a sponge.

If you walked on the moon without a spacesuit you would get badly sunburnt within a few seconds. Luckily, our planet's atmosphere stops us from burning so quickly.

The people of Kathmandu were shocked when it snowed in February 2007 – it hadn't snowed there for 63 years!

The male mistle thrush senses when bad weather is coming and sings from the top of a tree or rooftop. It used to be known as a *stormcock*.

Oak trees don't produce acorns until they are 50 years old.

A *lungfish* can live out of water for up to four years! During dry seasons, it burrows into mud and breathes through a pair of basic lungs.

At least 90 per cent of plants depend on fungi for their survival.

Dinosaurs roamed the earth for more than 100 million years.

A million meteors enter the Earth's atmosphere every day! Luckily, most of them are only the size of a grain of sand.

Most people stay as far away as possible from a tornado, but cinematographer Sean Casey wants to sit inside one. He has built an armour-plated Tornado Intercept Vehicle so that he can film a direct hit from a tornado and record its speed.

Potassium chloride is used to stop the heart during cardiac surgery.

Atoms are particles so tiny that 4,000 million would fit on this full stop.

New uniforms for the police in Gujarat, India, are impregnated with a permanent fresh flower and citrus fragrance. The latest fibre optic technology means they can also be seen in the dark!

Light is the fastest thing in the universe and travels at more than 300,000 kilometres (180,000 miles) per hour.

Earmuffs were invented by a 15-year-old American boy in the nineteenth century!

Researchers have monitored the movements of bees by attaching tiny barcodes to them.

Some types of bamboo can grow 90 centimetres (3 feet) in a day. You can almost see them growing!

In electronics, a jiffy is one sixtieth of a second.

Tropical cloud forests are shrouded in mist most of the time. The lack of sunlight means that trees tend to be shorter than in rainforests and the ground is covered in moss.

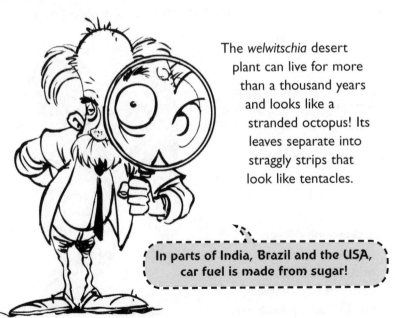

The *welwitschia* desert plant can live for more than a thousand years and looks like a stranded octopus! Its leaves separate into straggly strips that look like tentacles.

In parts of India, Brazil and the USA, car fuel is made from sugar!

Sand is mostly made from tiny pieces of the mineral *quartz*.

American engineer Percy Spencer invented the microwave oven after a chocolate bar melted in his pocket as he stood next to a radar tube.

The first traffic lights were manually operated red and green gaslights, placed outside London's Houses of Parliament. Unfortunately, they exploded and injured the policeman who was operating them.

The largest volcano is in Hawaii. It's more than 15 kilometres (9 miles) high, with its base in the sea.

It takes one day for the Earth to rotate once on its axis. It does not last 24 hours, but 23 hours and 56 minutes!

Siamese kittens are cream in colour. As they grow, the coolest parts of the body darken, due to an enzyme in their hair that is heat-activated.

The daytime temperature on Mercury is about 430 degrees Celsius (806 degrees Fahrenheit). That's hot!

Drips of molten glass cooled in water form tadpole-shaped glass drops that shatter into a powder if the 'tail' is tweaked. They are known as *Prince Rupert's Drops* after their inventor Prince Rupert of the Rhine, who used them to play jokes.

You can be struck by lightning even if you are indoors! A bolt can travel down phone lines, electric cables and plumbing pipes, so keep away from them during an electrical storm.

When bacteria were first discovered they were named *animalcules*.

Water is 9 per cent lighter when it's frozen – that's why your ice cubes float.

Virga is rain that evaporates before it reaches the ground.

Baikal seals can be found only in Lake Baikal, Siberia. The lake is a long way from the ocean, so how they got there is a scientific mystery!

Sapphires can be brown, clear, grey or black, as well as blue.

The leaf of the giant Amazon water lily is so strong that you could sit on it without sinking!

It takes Saturn more than 29 years to orbit the sun.

A Tyrannosaurus rex was so heavy that if it fell over, it would have died from the impact. Those little arms were no good for breaking its fall either!

Ultraviolet light from the sun has antiseptic properties. It causes sunburn, too!

The world's first hydroelectric power station used water from a lake to light a country house in Northumberland, England, in 1870.

Silver conducts heat and electricity more quickly than any other metal.

Mad Serbian scientist Nikola Tesla was obsessed with the number three: he would have to walk round the block three times before entering a building and insisted that the number of any hotel room he stayed in be divisible by three.

The Ginkgo tree is a *living fossil* – that means it is a unique tree with no close living relatives and dates back 270 million years.

Young green tree pythons are yellow, red or brown!

In 1930, a University of Queensland professor began an experiment with a funnel full of pitch (tar) to show his students how something that appears solid can be a liquid. The first drip took ten years to fall and the eighth drip fell in 2000. It will be a hundred years before all the pitch has dripped through, finishing the long, long experiment!

It rains at the same time every day in rainforests on the equator.

Some bacteria are sensitive to the Earth's magnetic field. *Magnetotactic bacteria* all point to *magnetic north*.

80 per cent of the world's deserts are not sandy but rocky. Some are salt-covered and a few are even icy.

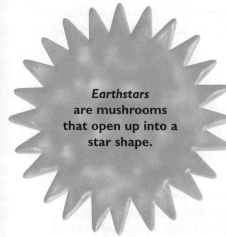

Earthstars are mushrooms that open up into a star shape.

You're electric! Your nervous system is constantly sending messages around the body by electrical impulses.

A British scientist decided to take his four children on a trek up part of Mount Everest to research how their bodies coped with low oxygen levels. That's one way to earn your pocket money, kids…

The first raincoats designed by Charles Macintosh were made waterproof with rubber and a by-product of coal tar. They kept people dry but the smell was horrid!

Raindrops are not teardrop-shaped: small ones are spherical and larger ones are flat on the bottom – kind of burger-bun shaped!

The people of Siberia were surprised when they looked out one morning and saw a blanket of…orange snow! The reason for the freaky colour remained a mystery, but it was believed to have been caused by pollution.

The World Wide Web was born in 1991. There are now over 1,000 million internet users globally!

Gold is the softest metal – a traditional test was to bite it and see if the teeth left a mark.

Finland has 187,888 lakes and 179,584 islands.

Until the 15th century, Christian scholars believed that Jerusalem was the centre of the universe and that the Earth was a flat disc surrounded by oceans.

Diamonds are so hard that only other diamonds can scratch them.

The first alarm clocks were created for monks in the 14th century to make sure they didn't miss their morning prayers!

Less than 1 per cent of all the water on our planet is drinkable.

The planet Mars was named after the Roman god of war because it looks red – the colour of blood.

It takes ten minutes for rain to drip through the dense leaves of a rainforest and reach the forest floor.

The dodo bird was made extinct only 80 years after it was discovered.

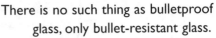

American scientist Benjamin Franklin had bad eyesight and got so fed up of switching between different pairs of spectacles that he invented bifocals!

There is no such thing as bulletproof glass, only bullet-resistant glass. One-way bullet-resistant glass has recently been invented for armoured vehicles, protecting the occupants but allowing them to defend themselves.

A third of the world's population is infected with tuberculosis (TB) – one person per second picks up the bacteria. Some people carry TB but do not become ill from it themselves.

Chalk is made from the fossilized skeletons of tiny sea animals!

The Eiffel Tower is painted in three different colours! Because of the effects of light and background, three shades are needed to make it appear to be one colour.

The ten highest mountains in the world are all in the Himalayas.

Some rocks can float! In a volcanic eruption, the violent separation of gas from lava produces a 'frothy' rock called *pumice*, which is loaded with gas bubbles.

Flash floods and landslides unearthed an ancient tree trunk in Switzerland. The white pine trunk, believed to have been preserved in ice, was examined by experts and found to be 2,815 years old!

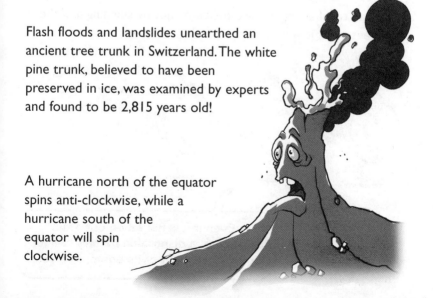

A hurricane north of the equator spins anti-clockwise, while a hurricane south of the equator will spin clockwise.

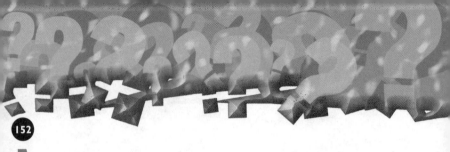

Yucca plants and yucca moths depend on each other for survival – the small moth is the only creature that can pollinate the plants as it feeds.

Pure water is a light shade of blue.

Every rainbow is unique: each rainbow is formed from light hitting your eye at a very precise angle. Someone standing next to you will see light coming from a slightly different angle than you and therefore see a different rainbow.

You can tell if an egg is hard-boiled or not by spinning it: if the inside is solid, it will carry on spinning. If the egg is raw, the liquid contents will stop the egg spinning within three rotations.

Even if it is not taken out of its packaging, a disposable battery will lose up to 25 per cent of its power in a year.

There are earthquakes on the moon…called moonquakes, of course! There are also icequakes in Antarctica.

The cracks in breaking glass travel at more than 5,000 kilometres (3,000 miles) per hour.

There are more than 150 giant craters around the world, left by fallen meteorites. The largest one is in Arizona, USA – it measures more than 1,200 metres (4,000 feet) in diameter and was created around 50,000 years ago.

Water can cut through steel! Waterjet tools shoot water through a fine nozzle at such a high pressure that the jet cuts metal – and it never needs sharpening.

German scientists Josef von Mering and Oskar Minkowski discovered diabetes when, out of curiosity, they removed the pancreas from a dog and monitored the effects.

Diamond dust is a kind of glittering polar fog made up of tiny ice crystals.

Nineteenth-century British chemist Humphry Davy was addicted to *nitrous oxide* – laughing gas!

Iron and sulphur compounds are present in eggs – if you hard-boil one for too long, they will show up as a green coating around the yolk.

In the middle of the Atlantic, the two plates – the African plate and the American plate – are moving apart at about the same speed as your fingernails grow.

Uranus was originally called the *Georgian Planet,* after King George III.

Salt and vinegar is an explosive combination! There is a spectacular chemical reaction when the two are mixed in large quantities. Don't try it yourself, though...

The Earth is travelling through space at an astonishing 108,000 kilometres (65,000 miles) per hour!

Burning potassium gives off a violet flame.

Italian genius Leonardo da Vinci was a very busy man – as well as being a painter and inventor, he was an engineer, anatomist, architect, astronomer, musician, scientist, sculptor, mathematician and writer!

The largest, heaviest land animal that ever lived was the *Argentinosaurus*. It grew up to 35 metres (115 feet) long and weighed 80-100 tonnes.

There are a million bacteria in a millilitre of fresh water.

A total solar eclipse can be seen from the same place only once every 370 years.

Stainless steel and water can neutralise strong odours such as garlic and fish. Soap-shaped pieces of steel are available, but a spoon is just as effective!

The poison *arsenic* occurs naturally throughout the earth's crust and can pollute drinking water.

The moon used to be much closer to our planet than it is now! A billion years ago, it would take only 20 days to go round the Earth, compared to the 27 days it takes now. It's still moving away by about 4 centimetres (1.5 inches) a year.

Despite being as big as several countries, China has only one time zone. Until 1949, it had five.

The biggest stars in the galaxy are called *supergiants* and *hypergiants*. A red *supergiant* can be 1,500 times bigger than the sun!

Venus is shrouded in clouds of sulphur dioxide and sulphuric acid.

An oily plant substance called *petrichor* is what causes the refreshing smell after rainfall. Plants secrete it during dry periods and the scent is released when it rains.

The hagfish secretes a unique slimy mucus – it is reinforced with fine, strong fibres similar to spider silk.

Long before Alexander Fleming discovered penicillin, ancient Egyptians and ancient Greeks recognised that some moulds had antibacterial properties and used them for dressing wounds.

1001 Unbelievable Facts

Migrating birds are sensitive to the earth's magnetic field and use it to guide them during their flights.

Beer Crater on Mars is named after German astronomer Wilhelm Beer.

There were no polar ice caps 90 million years ago and Alaska was as warm as southern California is now!

Baobab trees, also known as monkey bread trees, can store up to 120,000 litres (253,605 pints) of water in their trunks! This is to make sure they survive during long droughts.

Most colours have a wavelength, but brown doesn't. It's just a combination of other colours and their wavelengths.

Unbelievable
World
Record
Facts

CAUTION: Some of these World Record Facts include dangerous activities. They have been set by people who have had proper medical guidance. Don't try any of them at home!

Sultan Hassanal Bolkiah of Brunei has the largest collection of Rolls-Royces, owning around 150. He has 2,000 other luxury cars, too!

Kilauea in Hawaii is the world's most active volcano and has been erupting non-stop since 1983.

American Ashrita Furman broke the fastest skipping record in 2007 by skipping 5 kilometres (3.1 miles) in 35 minutes 19 seconds. He skipped at Tiger Temple in Thailand…and had a tiger trotting alongside him most of the way!

The youngest person to reach the top of Mount Everest was 15-year-old Ming Kipa Sherpa in 2003.

The box jellyfish is the most venomous type, with a sting that can kill in 4 minutes.

Joss Stone was the youngest BRIT Award winner when she won two awards aged 18 in 2005.

Astronomers spotted the fastest star in the galaxy in 2005. It was zooming through the Milky Way at more than 2.4 million kilometres (1.5 million miles) per hour!

The only known koala twins were born in 1999 in Queensland.

250,000 brightly coloured power balls were used for the Sony Bravia TV advertisement, the most props ever used in a commercial.

The world's tallest building is Taipei 101 in Taiwan, which stands 508 metres(1,666 feet) high.

The bee hummingbird is the smallest bird, with the male measuring just 57 millimetres (2.24 inches) in length.

Russia has a record 15,000 circus artists.

The largest insectivore is the moon rat – a kind of hedgehog! Its full length is around 60 centimetres (2 feet).

The largest meteorite from Mars weighed 18 kilograms (40 pounds) and landed in Nigeria.

The longest cuddle ever lasted for 5,000 years! Archaeologists discovered a pair of entwined skeletons in Northern Italy and believe the couple to be from the Neolithic period.

A record number of 269 Asian elephants gathered to eat over 50 tonnes (11,231 pounds) of fruit and vegetables at Thailand's 2003 annual elephant parade.

The world's smallest owl is the elf owl – it's the same size as a sparrow!

There are places on Earth that are covered in salt! The largest salt flats are in Bolivia, where 10 billion tonnes of salt cover an area of 12,000 square kilometres (4,600 square miles).

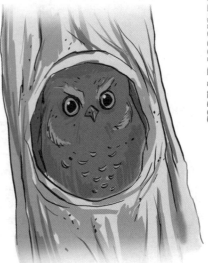

The youngest FIFA World Cup Final scorer is Pelé, who was just 17 when he scored for Brazil in 1958.

How many Australians can you get on a surfboard? Forty-seven on a specially designed one, and they all rode a wave on it!

The smallest spy plane is not much bigger than your hand! The *Black Widow* was developed to carry a miniature video camera.

The USA has the largest air force in the world, with more than 6,000 aircraft.

The longest ever backwards motorcycle journey was completed by a group of 14 members of the Swedish Army Lions motorcycle display team. They rode their Husaberg 400cc bikes backwards for a distance of 17.5 km (10.87 miles) in aid of the 600th anniversary of their town, Skövde.

The world's biggest aquarium opened in 2005 in Atlanta. The Georgia Aquarium contains more than 100,000 sea creatures.

Creme Puff the cat lived to the ripe old age of 38 years and 3 days! That is nearly 350 cat years!

At the age of 22, Fernando Alonso became the youngest driver to win a Formula One World Championship race when he won the 2003 Hungarian Grand Prix.

The oldest person to grow a new tooth was 61.

Thieves staged the largest ever jewel robbery when they got away with $100 million (£62 million) worth of gems from the Antwerp Diamond Centre in 2003.

Hurricane Wilma was the strongest ever, with wind speeds reaching 270 kilometres (165 miles) per hour.

The longest word in the English language is the name of a lung disease called *pneumonoultramicroscopicsilicovolcano-coniosis*.

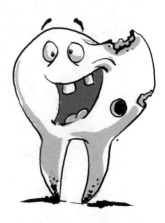

Dr Who is the longest-running science fiction TV series. The BBC broadcast the first episode in 1963.

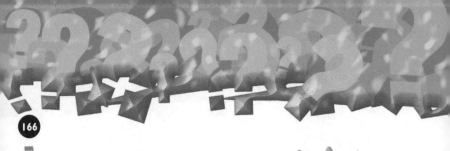

The fastest tennis serve came from American Andy Roddick and was measured at 246.2 kilometres (153 miles) per hour.

Three children in the Norwegian Henriksen family were born four years apart on a Leap Day (29th February).

American Richard Presley lived in an underwater module for 69 days and 19 minutes as part of research into the effects of living under the sea.

Northern Irish men have the highest rate of heart disease in the world.

Daredevil Stephen Brown rode a motorcycle through a tunnel of fire that was 51 metres (167 feet) long.

American cyclist Scott Koons cycled 21.16 kilometres (13.15 miles) round a track with no hands. Hasn't anyone told him that's dangerous?

North and South America make up the largest area of land named after one person – 15th-century Italian explorer Amerigo Vespucci.

Addwaitya the giant tortoise was the world's oldest animal! He died in India at the grand old age of 255 and his 1.5 metre (5 feet) wide shell later went on display at a local museum.

The biggest recorded meteor shower fell over the Pacific Ocean in 1966, when 40,000 shooting stars shot across the sky in 20 minutes.

The gecko is the only lizard that makes noises.

German man Johann Traber performed the fastest motorcycle wheelie on a tightrope in 2005 by travelling at 53 kilometres (32 miles) per hour!

The world's longest banana split was more than 7 kilometres (4 miles) long!

Steve Griffiths and Philip John have both been bog-snorkelling world champions three times.

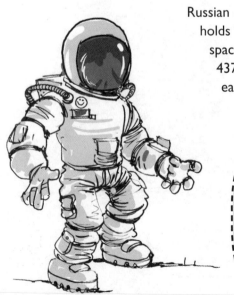

Russian cosmonaut Valeriy Polyakov holds the record for the longest spaceflight in history – he spent 437 days in space and orbited the earth more than 7,000 times!

The most brightly coloured dolphin is the Chinese pink dolphin. Its colour comes from the large number of blood vessels near the surface of its skin.

The world's first female prime minister was Sri Lankan Sirimavo Bandaranaike, who took office in 1960.

A watermelon is 92 per cent water – the highest percentage of any fruit.

Surinam in South America has the fewest cinemas per population – one cinema between more than 436,000 people!

Speed skater Jiajun Li from China took just 1 minute 24 seconds to get round a 1000-metre (3280 feet) track in 2004.

The *bunchberry dogwood* flower opens its petals in 0.5 milliseconds!

The shark's sense of smell is greater than any other fish – it can detect one part of blood in 100 million parts of water.

The wettest place on Earth is the Indian town of Cherrapunji, with an average annual rainfall of 11.43 metres (38 feet 2 inches).

A record 2,844 kilograms (6,272 pounds) of plasticine was used to make Aardman Animation's *Wallace and Gromit: Curse of the Were-Rabbit*.

More than 200 million people have visited the Eiffel Tower since it was built, making it the world's most visited monument.

The largest pink lake is in Senegal and measures 1.5 x 5 kilometres (1 x 3 miles). Its colour comes from minerals and micro-organisms.

Spiders Arabella and Anita were the first to spin webs in space in 1973!

Sir Don Bradman (Australia) and Brian Lara (Trinidad and Tobago) are the only two batsmen in Test match cricket to have scored two innings of more than 300 runs.

The USA produces more household waste per person than any other nation.

The *howler monkey* is the loudest land animal – its call can be heard more than 5 kilometres (3 miles) away. The red howler monkey is the noisiest!

The fastest carrot chopper in the West is British TV chef James Martin – he peeled and chopped 515 grams (18 ounces) in one minute!

The worst air-show disaster happened in 2002, when a fighter jet crashed into spectators in Ukraine and killed 78 people, injuring more than 100.

French skater Stephane Alfano performed a record 16 consecutive flatspins on inline skates in 2005.

The Jamaican iguana is the rarest lizard, with around only 100 in existence.

The largest living structure on earth is the Great Barrier Reef in Australia – it's over 2,000 kilometres (1,200 miles) long!

The heaviest object ever weighed was a launch pad Revolving Service Structure at NASA's Kennedy Space Center in Florida. The RSS weighed 2,423 tonnes (5,342,000 pounds).

The longest TV advert was for Lipton Ice Tea Green and lasted a snoozy 24 minutes.

German golfers Eric Kirchner and Patrick Herrresthal played six rounds of golf in six different countries in one day!

The youngest person to reach the South Pole was 18-year-old Sarah Ann McNair-Landry in 2005.

Adám Lörincz was the world's youngest musical composer at 14 years 76 days when his musical, *Star of the King*, was performed on August 16, 2002 in Hungary.

American Mike 'Rooftop' Escamilla holds the record for the longest BMX back flip at a distance of 18.94 metres (62 feet 2 inches).

Top Dubai chefs made a date and banana cake that stretched along the seafront for 2,530 metres (8,303 feet) in 1996.

The *Arctic tern* has the longest migration of any bird – it breeds in the Arctic, flies south to Antarctica during the northern winter, then flies back again!

Russia has 11 time zones, more than any other country.

Chelsea FC player Frank Lampard played in a record 160 consecutive Premiership matches.

The world's largest ice hotel is in Sweden and is built every year in December.

The fastest production car is the Bugatti Veyron, which can be driven at speeds of more than 400 kilometres (248 miles) per hour.

The largest ocean is the Pacific – it makes up 45.9 per cent of the world's oceans.

The world's most premature surviving baby was Amillia Taylor, who was just the length of a ballpoint pen when she was born at less than 22 weeks.

The longest earthquake lasted for ten minutes in the Sumatra-Andaman Islands.

German racing driver Michael Schumacher holds two world records: he has won the most Grand Prix races (83) and the most World Championships in Formula One (7).

A US restaurant produced the world's biggest burger for a charity event. It contained a 48-kilogram (80 pound) beef patty and 160 cheese slices!

Enormous hailstones caused around $1 billion (£620 million) worth of damage during a 1984 storm in Munich, making it the worst damage toll from a hailstorm.

The highest internet café in the world is at Mount Everest base camp, more than 5,000 metres (16,600 feet) above sea level.

The smallest animal trained to detect landmines is the honeybee!

American Timothy Turner Hayes had skied on every continent except Antarctica by the age of 14.

Edinburgh chip shop owner Selim Sener set a world record when he wrapped 10 portions of chips in one minute for a National Chip Week event.

Athletes Justin Gatlin (USA) and Asafa Powell (Jamaica) have both run the 100 metres race in 9.77 seconds. See how quickly you can do it!

The world's leading ice cream eaters are the Australians, scoffing 16.6 litres (3.6 gallons) per person each year.

Dallas golden retriever Augie could hold five tennis balls in his mouth at once!

The largest hoard of coins was discovered in 1908, when 150,000 13th-century coins were unearthed in Belgium.

The noisiest spider is the European buzzing spider. The male makes a buzzing sound as it vibrates its abdomen against a leaf to attract a mate.

Jupiter is the largest planet in the solar system; it's more than 300 times bigger than the Earth!

US rapper 50 Cent had a record three singles in the US Top 5 in 2005: *Candy Shop, How We Do* and *Disco Inferno*.

The largest toothpick sculpture was Alligator Alley, made by American Michael Smith from more than 3 million toothpicks!

The puma is known by 40 different names, the most for any animal.

Karen Davies of Britain has won the toe wrestling World Championships a record four times.

The fastest lava flow burst from Nyiragongo in the Democratic Republic of Congo at 60 kilometres (40 miles) per hour.

Japan's *Big O* is the world's first centreless Ferris wheel. It has Tokyo's biggest roller coaster running right through it.

In 2005, Hans Van Dan Helzen from the US completed 51 yo-yo tricks in one minute!

The highest temperature recorded in the shade was 58 degrees Celsius (136 degrees Fahrenheit) at Al 'Aziziyah in Libya. That was in 1922, before anyone had even heard of global warming!

Astronaut Helen Sharman was the first Briton in space in 1991.

American Dale Webster surfed every day between 2nd September 1975 and 29th February 2004, clocking up a record 10,407 consecutive days of surfing. Awesome!

Brazilian star striker Ronaldo has scored 15 World Cup Final goals.

The *sailfish* can whizz along at a record speed of 100 kilometres (60 miles) per hour.

American Ron Scarpa has been barefoot water-skiing World Champion four times. Water-skiing barefoot is an achievement in itself!

Canada's Rideau Canal Skateway is 7.8 kilometres (4.8 miles) long and is the largest naturally frozen ice rink.

Australian Kay Cottee was the first woman to sail around the world solo and non-stop in 1988.

The dumbo octopus, so-called because of its flapping frills that look like an elephant's ears, lives deeper in the ocean than any other at 1,500 metres (5,000 feet).

The lowest temperature endured by a bird is minus 20 degrees Celsius (minus 4 degrees Fahrenheit), the Antarctic chill felt by Emperor penguins.

Puck the budgie knew a record 1,728 words before he died in 1994.

American Gary Duschl has been collecting gum wrappers for more than 40 years. He has linked together more than a million wrappers to make a record-breaking chain that is more than 14,000 metres (45,000 feet) long!

American Milburn Hart did a parachute jump at the age of 96 years 63 days. It's never too late!

Wacky scientist Nikola Tesla created the longest man-made bolt of lightning in his lab in 1899. It was 40 metres (130 feet) long and could be heard for miles.

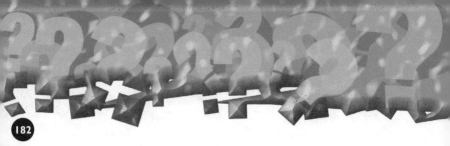

The longest wall is the Great Wall of China. At 3,460 kilometres (2,150 miles), it is three times the length of Britain.

Kathryn Ratcliffe ate 170 Smarties in 3 minutes…using chopsticks. You can try that one at home!

The carnivorous plants that devour the largest prey are from the *Nepenthacae* family. The Asian rainforest plants can digest frogs, birds and rats.

The largest kangaroo is as tall as a man! The red kangaroo can be up to 5 feet 11 inches (1.8 metres) tall.

The smallest nest is built by the vervain hummingbird and is the size of half a walnut shell!

The most heat-tolerant organism lives in the boiling hot hydrothermal vents at the bottom of the Pacific Ocean. Bacteria-like *Strain 121* can survive temperatures of 121 degrees Celsius (250 degrees Fahrenheit).

Uruguay man Emilio Arenas Florin began collecting key rings in 1955 and now has more than 25,630!

Ashrita Furman of the US jumped 37.18 kilometres (23.11 miles) on a pogo stick in 1997.

In 2003, American Jay Stokes made 534 parachute jumps in 24 hours. That's a jump every 2.5 minutes and a lot of them were in the rain!

The oldest playable instrument is a 9,000-year-old Chinese flute, made from a bird's leg bone.

The fastest FIFA World Cup sending-off went to Uruguayan player José Batista, 56 seconds into the 1986 match against Scotland.

The world's longest hot dog was 17.5 metres (57 feet 4 inches) long!

Pharaoh Phiops II ruled for a record 94 years from the age of 6.

Australian Kareena Oates set the hula hooping world record in 2005, with 100 hoops at once. See how many you can manage!

The oldest commissioned warship still afloat is the USS Constitution, which has been part of the US Navy since 1797.

The Japanese are the biggest comic readers. Their *manga* comics account for 40 per cent of all printed material sold.

The African *patas* monkey can race along the ground at 55 kilometres (34 miles) an hour, making it the fastest primate.

The deepest half marathon took place in a Polish salt mine at a depth of 212 metres (695 feet).

The highest number of international goals scored by a female football player is 144, by American Mia Hamm.

US astronauts Eugene Cernan and Harrison Schmitt took the longest moon walk in 1972. They spent more than seven hours outside their module and explored 20.4 kilometres (12.6 miles) of the moon's surface.

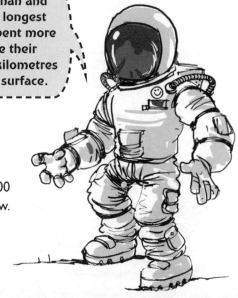

The largest number of living creatures produced during a magic performance was 80,000 bees in a Penn and Teller show.

The largest set of Russian nesting dolls (*matrioshkas*) contained 51 pieces that were hand painted by artist Youlia Bereznitskaya. The smallest doll was just 3 millimetres (0.12 inches) high!

The first Olympic Games was held in 776 BC.

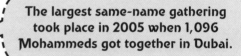

The largest same-name gathering took place in 2005 when 1,096 Mohammeds got together in Dubai.

Peter Jackson's third *The Lord of the Rings* film, *The Return of the King* won a record 11 Oscars.

The *peacock mantis* shrimp has the strongest animal punch! Its front leg moves at 23 metres (75 feet) per second to club its prey.

Louisiana's Second Lake Pontchartrain Causeway is the world's longest bridge at 38.4 kilometres (23.8 miles) long. If you stand in the middle of it, you cannot see either end!

The youngest person to visit the wreck of the *Titanic* was 13-year-old Sebastian Harris in 2005.

Australian Minnie Munro became the oldest bride when she got married at the age of 102.

The American *Achaearenea tepidariorium* spider has the strongest known web, tough enough to ensnare a mouse.

Mandarin Chinese is the most popular spoken language in the world, with 915 million speakers.

Nineteen scuba divers took part in the largest underwater cycle race in Guernsey in 2005.

Elvis Presley is the richest dead celebrity. He earned $45 million (£26 million) in 2005 alone.

Britons lead the world in baked bean consumption! They eat 5.3 kilograms (11 pounds 10 ounces) per person per year – about four times more than people in the USA!

As part of his job, American W.R. 'Rusty' Haight was a human crash-test dummy in a record 718 collisions.

The longest non-stop commercial airline flight was from Hong Kong to London and took 22 hours and 42 minutes.

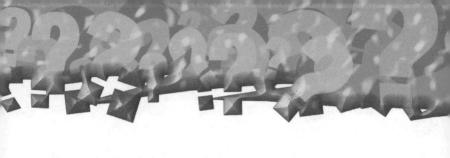

Unbelievable
Random Facts

A shortsighted Croatian granddad sparked a police manhunt when he went to collect his grandson from nursery…and took the wrong boy home!

The Empire State Building is struck by lightning about 100 times every year.

Second World War veteran Don Karkos had been blind for 64 years after receiving a shrapnel wound. His sight was miraculously restored when he was head-butted by the racehorse he was looking after!

There are no donkeys in the Donkey Kong computer game.

Carhenge on the Nebraska plains is a replica of England's Stonehenge…made with 38 vintage cars that are painted grey!

There are more than 32,000 radio stations around the world.

Fake snow used to be made from asbestos, so people would have sprinkled the toxic mineral around their homes!

Hawaiians consume more Spam than anyone else in the world.

A Swiss pilot designed wings and jet engines that could be strapped to his back and allow him to fly. He couldn't run fast enough to take off, though – he had to jump from an airborne aeroplane!

Cop is short for *constable on patrol.*

Watermelon snow is found in California's Sierra Nevada. Algae make it pink and it smells of watermelon too!

Some twins create their own language, known as *cryptophasia,* that only they can understand.

A sick Yorkshire Terrier was found by a vet to have swallowed eight party balloons. After they were removed, it must have felt a little deflated!

Blue *snow fleas* can be spotted hopping around on the snow on a winter's day.

Bao Xishun, the world's tallest man, saved the lives of two dolphins in 2006 by reaching into their stomachs with his long arms, which measure 1.06 metres (42 inches), and removing pieces of plastic.

Attempting to go over Niagara Falls is illegal. Several people have been drowned or injured doing so.

A crazy Romanian man named his baby daughter after one of his favourite Mercedes cars: SLK. If he'd had a boy, he would have named him BMW!

Japanese kimono-makers don't just throw away their broken needles; they hold a special festival for them! During *hari-kuyo*, the women thank the needles for their hard work and place them in a slab of tofu.

A British survey of 2,000 people showed that more men than women take a cuddly toy to bed with them.

Stewardesses is the longest word that can be typed using just the left hand part of a computer keyboard.

Australian banknotes are waterproof.

Red rain fell in the Indian state of Kerala in 2001. The reason for the strange colour is still a mystery, but theories range from algae spores or pollution to the blood of bats or extraterrestrials!

The Japanese believe that a clean toilet brings good fortune. They even have books on the subject!

The Eiffel Tower sways up to 7 centimetres (almost 3 inches) in the wind.

More than 25 per cent of the world's natural gas reserves are in Russia.

A great-grandmother outdid her fishing champion husband on a family holiday in Florida by catching a shark 2.7 metres (9 feet) long!

Al Capone's business card said he was a used furniture dealer.

Australia has a plague of poisonous cane toads, which can grow to be the size of a small dog. The government has asked people to kill them humanely, but most Australians just bash them over the head!

The name for the Volkswagen Beetle in Bulgarian translates as *Volkswagen Turtle*.

A Japanese man was so angry at a new building blocking out his light that he shot it, causing lots of damage and getting himself arrested!

The US Mint discovered that the words *In God We Trust* were missing from some of their $1 coins in 2007. Since coins with faults are valuable to collectors, one was sold on eBay for $405 (£206)!

A fighter jet and a surface-to-air missile were put up for sale on a Chinese auction website. You really can buy anything on the internet!

The average person spends two years of his or her life on the telephone.

Helium is made up of the tiniest possible particles that can escape easily – that's why your balloons go down so quickly!

188 million Valentine's cards are exchanged every year.

Voice actor Mel Blanc was known as *the man of a thousand voices,* but he denied this – he said he had provided only 850! His most famous characters were Bugs Bunny and Daffy Duck.

Advertising which targets children under the age of 12 is banned in Sweden.

Many types of trees benefit from forest fires and some need them to regenerate.

A Bosnian man faked his own death to see who would attend his funeral. Only his mother showed up!

A Serbian footballer who was dropped from his club got his own back by churning up the pitch with a tractor.

150 saffron crocuses are needed to produce 1 gram of the spice saffron.

Satellite navigation systems can't always be trusted. Drivers following instructions have ended up in the river in a little village in Wiltshire, England, and now locals are charging £25 ($49) to pull them out!

The word for taxi is the same in 13 languages.

A Nebraska man saved his dog with the kiss of life after it fell into an icy lake whilst chasing geese.

It took 14 years to build the Sydney Opera House.

The population of the world is 6.6 billion – more than 203,000 babies are born every day!

The largest charity donation in American history is $30 billion (£17 billion), given by businessman and philanthropist Warren Buffet to the Bill and Melinda Gates Foundation.

The Sargasso Sea has no coastline – it's in the middle of the North Atlantic Ocean.

Johnny Herbert came fifth in the 1989 United States Grand Prix, but a local American firm refused him a hire car because he was under 25.

Only three cricketers have ever scored the maximum of 36 runs in an over – Garfield Sobers in 1968, Ravi Shastri in 1985 and Herschelle Gibbs in 2007.

As Jonny Wilkinson scored the goal that sent the England rugby team to World Cup victory in 2003, his mum was out shopping at her local supermarket!

The first item ever to have its barcode scanned was a pack of chewing gum.

It is illegal to keep a gerbil as a pet in California, since gerbils have been known to carry tuberculosis.

A Chinese couple were in such a rush to meet relatives that they left their 3-year-old son behind on the plane!

You took your life in your hands playing American Football in its formative years. In the 1905 season, 18 players were killed and 150 seriously injured.

50,000 text messages are sent every minute around the world.

Japan has the highest number of vending machines: one for every 23 people. They sell anything from live lobsters to potted plants!

Snap, crackle, pop in German is *knisper, knasper, knusper!*

College lecturer Paul Rogerson creates award-winning sculptures…from lard! His works of characters from Bugs Bunny to Don Quijote last only two months before they go off and become a bit stinky.

There are around 1,250 Boeing 737s in the air around the world at any one time.

A Mexican postman was arrested after police officers found 10 tonnes of undelivered letters at his house.

A beauty contest for pensioners has been launched in Switzerland…called Miss Retirement Home! Plans are now underway for a Mr Retirement Home competition.

The Chicago River is dyed green every year to celebrate St Patrick's Day.

An elderly woman who died in the economy section of an aeroplane shortly after take-off was moved to first class for the remainder of the long flight. The things people will do to get an upgrade…

Pablo Picasso, Leonardo da Vinci and Paul McCartney all have roses named after them.

Saw-scaled vipers make a sizzling sound.

More than 700 languages are spoken in Indonesia.

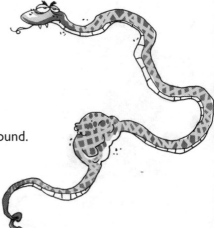

An American who had his glasses broken and eye bruised by a snowball decided to sue the thrower for more than $3,800 (£2,000). Snow joke!

It is offensive for an Inuit person to be called an Eskimo.

Parachutes have a hole in the top! The modern design lets built-up air through, which in old parachutes used to cause a swinging motion.

Police in Soweto were called out to deal with attacks on pedestrians…by giant rats! The scary rodents were nesting in old cars and protested if people passed by.

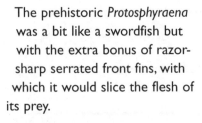

The prehistoric *Protosphyraena* was a bit like a swordfish but with the extra bonus of razor-sharp serrated front fins, with which it would slice the flesh of its prey.

A Cologne couple were locked inside a cinema for the night after they fell asleep during a film.

There are three golf balls on the moon.

The first cash machine was installed in a New York bank in 1939, but taken out six months later because customers didn't like it. There were no more for 25 years after that!

A British man blinded in an accident had his sight restored nine years later when he was struck by lightning.

There were no vehicles on Pitcairn Island in the South Pacific until the early 1970s.

The Palanga Amber Museum in Lithuania has a collection of around 28,000 pieces of amber, half of which contain fossilized insects, spiders or plants.

In the USA, more than 150 pairs of identical twins are married to identical twins!

Bookkeeper is the only word in the English language with three sets of double letters together.

Ice hockey was invented in Montreal in 1875.

A day (sunrise to sunrise) on the planet Mercury is longer than a year (one orbit around the sun).

Buddhist monks refused to kill any of the ants infesting their Kuala Lumpur temple because of their beliefs in non-violence... even when one monk was hospitalized by ant bites!

Of the 40 horses that began the 2001 Grand National horse race in England, only two finished without stopping.

Beards are banned by the US Army and Marine Corps.

Bulgarian-American singer Bantcho Bantchevsky is most famous for killing himself during the interval of an opera by jumping off a balcony at the Metropolitan Opera House in New York.

Indian Yellow paint pigment was originally made from the dried urine of cows that had been fed on only mango leaves and water.

A man was banned from a pub in Scotland…because he kept doing smelly farts!

If you multiply 21978 by 4, the number you get is its mirror image – 87912. Try it and see!

An Israeli plane was delayed when a little bird flew into the cockpit as passengers were boarding. The passengers had to leave the plane and wait several hours while a professional bird-catcher was called to remove it.

The first cup of coffee was drunk on the moon in 1969.

A middle-aged Chinese bachelor placed an advertisement asking for someone to share his grave – so he wouldn't be lonely inthe afterlife!

Some sniffer dogs can track down pirate CDs and DVDs – they are trained to detect the chemicals used to make them.

Real gold and silver are sometimes used to decorate sweets and desserts! One New York restaurant lists *Golden Opulence* on its menu, an ice-cream sundae covered in 23-carat edible gold leaf.

A golf ball has around 400 dimples on it. The dimples make the ball travel farther.

The Pentagon is the world's biggest office building and has six postcodes all to itself.

Velcro comes from the French words for velvet (*velours*) and hook (*crochet*). Its inventor got the idea from sticky burrs on his clothes after a walk!

Ancient Egyptians loved cats and would shave off their eyebrows to mourn the death of one.

Your 1001st Unbelievable Fact!

....
....
....
....
....
....
....
....
....

I, the undersigned, hereby confirm that these facts are even more unbelievable than stuff about bloodsucking bat bugs and horses with hayfever.

Signed: ....

Date: ....